Cinetek series

The Navigator: A Mediaeval Odyssey

John Downie

FLICKS BOOKS

A CIP catalogue record for this book is available from the British Library.

ISBN 0 948911 65 4

First published in 2000 by

Flicks Books
29 Bradford Road
Trowbridge
Wiltshire BA14 9AN
England
Tel +44 1225 767728
Fax +44 1225 760418
E-mail flicks.books@dial.pipex.com

Printed and bound in Great Britain by Antony Rowe Ltd.

Contents

By any stretch of the imagination, New Zealand is a remote location on the earth's surface, ocean-locked 1200 miles south-east of the Australian continent, geologically ancient and volcanically recent. The continual proximity of land with sea, the fast-descending rivers, and the high mountain ranges, together with many local variations in climate and vegetation, have created a fragmented and fragile environment for its historically very recent human presence – Polynesians first set foot on the land between 1000 and 1800 years ago, while it was "discovered" as a potential European destination as late as Cook's first voyage of 1769, and effectively settled, in a complex interfacing of Māori tribes and British (or "Pākehā"), only 100 years later. The evolution of modern New Zealanders has emphasised the toughness, resilience and pragmatic improvisation needed by a frontier people shaping a nation inside a very brief time-frame, and always in the face of loss, silence and solitude – lives suddenly far from homeland, from centre, Polynesian as much as European. Ancestors in either case are perceived as comparatively recent (Māori as descendants of a mythologised number of tribal canoes; Europeans as descendants of a variety of historical "fleets"), and genealogies and kin-groups are preciously remembered and celebrated.

As a New Zealand-born Pākehā artist, Vincent Ward naturally is heir to particular qualities of sensibility provided by both place and culture.[1] The geographical and environmental elements are plainly present in all his films to date as climates, landscapes, and epic struggles for survival. He titled his brief book of recollections *Edge of the Earth* (1990), recognising the ideas of periphery and distance. The son of a third-generation father of Irish descent and a first-generation German-Jewish mother, Ward grew up on a farm in the agricultural valley of the Wairarapa region north of Wellington, seeing in his parents' lives the struggle to forge a livelihood out of scrubland. "I was not a lonely child, but an alone child", he writes, and he talks of the "emotional intensity" which filled him in childhood, as well as contact with such rooted European stories as those of the Brothers

Grimm and Sir Walter Scott. These geographical and temperamental climates reached a mature articulation in his first feature film, *Vigil* (1984). He has mentioned the theme of childhood as a particular New Zealand preoccupation in its art, and suggests that "maybe we are attracted to the theme because New Zealand is so remote that when we venture into the world outside we do so as innocents". This wilful wandering, to and from peripheries and centres, between childhood and adulthood, allied to a certain quality of naïve expectation, reaches powerful expression in Ward's 1992 film *Map of the Human Heart*. Despite incessant peregrination, "[i]t is the country and the family and the people I come from that gives my stories shape. And that I cannot escape."

Much film theory and critical practice over the past 30 years has focused on representation and reception (spectatorship) as central issues within cultural exchange, largely subsuming to them, sometimes contemptuously, the sensibility of individual artists. Without doubt, filmmaking is a collective practice, a completed work expressing many kinds of creative contribution. And, without doubt, the reception of a film by an audience, both as individuals and as collectives, constructs the mosaic of meanings to be found within it. But there is still an innocence present within this concatenation of experience which resounds about the business of production and reception, and sometimes we catch forceful sight or sound of it: somebody speaking, somebody seeing. Even in the bland, self-serving 1990s, not all films are inscrutably proficient as commodity. It was the idea of the "auteur" which effectively kicked film theory and criticism into discursive life in the 1950s, both as an expression of the distinctive "high-art" aspiration within European cinema, and as explaining the creative tension to be found between director/writer and genre commodification of American studio-produced film in particular. On the back of the romantic conception of the individual artist struggling against all odds to realise visions provoked by both biographical fact and intentional aspiration, theory compromised the presence of the individual *director* into the indubitable fact of an individual *film*'s *mise en scène*.[2] However, with a filmmaker such as Vincent Ward, we have a punctilious, obsessive sensibility which labours to assert itself as something more than just good craftsman or virtuoso technician. His presence is palpably central to the entire fact of a film's life.[3] An approach to understanding *The Navigator: A Mediaeval Odyssey* (1988) therefore needs to recognise the identity of its prime author, where he comes from, and what, as "an alone child", he dreams about.[4]

A story

Griffin is a nine-year-old boy, a dreamer and visionary, living in a remote ore-mining village in the high moors of the north of England in the mid-14th century. His adult brother Connor finally returns to the village after more than a month away, and reports the rapid approach of the Black Death. Almost immediately, the villagers have to repel a boat-load of refugees on whose bodies are the marks of plague. As a result of panic, faith and Griffin's premonitory dreams of a great cathedral and city, a small party of villagers, led by Connor and Griffin, embark on a quest to reach the cathedral, and plant a copper cross on its topmost spire. For this symbolic gesture to prove efficacious, protecting the village against the plague, they must complete their task before the moon sets and dawn breaks. After labouring downwards into the bowels of the earth, with the assistance of a powerful mining engine that they have discovered on the way, the pilgrims break through the Earth, to a distant view of the promised city. Approaching it has its difficulties. The party is separated trying to cross what proves to be a modern urban motorway. Connor sets out on his own to locate the cathedral, while the others inadvertently come upon a foundry in a run-down industrial zone. Eventually, three workers there agree to cast the mould which the pilgrims have brought. The cross is forged in copper.

In their urgency, and in their renewed attempts to reach the cathedral, Griffin and two companions steal a boat and a horse. Out on the water, they are stalked by a black sea monster in the shape of a nuclear submarine. From their imperilled craft, on an opposite bank they see Connor being hurtled along, pinned to the front of a railway locomotive. Miraculously, they reach the shore once again, but the baffling signs that strike Griffin's eye, including multiple television images of the submarine and its captain in an arcade shop front, confuse his intuitive sense of the cathedral's direction, and his companions have to blindfold him.

Finally, arriving at the cathedral, they see that Connor is already up high, steering the roped cross up towards its appointed position. Griffin runs to climb and follow him, convinced by now, through a repeating series of visions, that Connor will fall to his death. At this moment, a rope frays and Connor tumbles down the spire-ladder, severely damaging it. By the time Griffin reaches him, it is apparent that only the boy will be able to climb to the top. This he does, dropping the cross into place. But, as bells begin to peal, announcing the triumph of the quest, he loses his grip. It is the boy, the navigator, who falls to his death.

The group of pilgrims find themselves back in the pit they initially descended, apparently having only travelled on the wings of Griffin's visionary narrative. The village celebrates their "return", with the news that all the omens are good, and there appear to be no signs of the plague. However, Griffin discovers buboes swelling under his arms, and he confronts Connor, whose body is revealed to have the healing scars of the plague. His brother, after all, has been the carrier of the disease into the village.

But in the dream of the pilgrimage only one died, and, as its final moments showed, it is Griffin who is to be the single victim. The film ends with Connor pushing Griffin's coffin away over the waters from the lake shore.

Production history

From inception to completion, *The Navigator* covered the period 1984-88. Ward himself has left a set of sharply-etched impressions of the making of the film in *Edge of the Earth*. Filmmaking, as Ward himself states, "is both an act of faith and a gigantic gamble", and stories which accompany the development and realisation of most films perpetually stress the compromises which tear at a project's heart, and the cruel realities of life "over budget and behind schedule". What is clear from the making of *The Navigator*, despite its epic proportions and military-type planning,[5] is just how bare-boned its eventual realisation was, reflecting the hand-to-mouth life of the apprentice filmmaker, with the circumstances of the film's imaginative genesis perfectly epitomising Ward's vagabonding lifestyle of the time.[6]

The script was developed by Ward and associates in Auckland, and taken up by producer John Maynard as a one-off independent project. Working from Auckland, pre-production commenced in mid-1986. The cathedral spire was constructed and other location work was about to begin when "unexpected tax changes scared off our major investors", and the finances fell through. Unable to move the project on from New Zealand, at their lowest ebb both Maynard and Ward decamped to Australia, Ward in Sydney doggedly continuing his storyboard "in a storage room filled with old scripts and letters in the flat of an actor friend", and Maynard, with a single suitcase and US$25 000 borrowed from a friend, convinced that the film could be an Australian-New Zealand co-production.[7]

This it proved to be. The actors recruited were a mixture of professional and untried – the most interesting of these, Noel Appleby, who played Ulf, worked for the Auckland City Council in the sewers, was 70 pounds overweight, suffered from emphysema, and had been warned by his doctor that he could die before the film was completed. And obsessively, Ward hunted for two years, visiting more than 1000 classrooms, to find the child actor, Hamish McFarlane, he needed for the lead.[8] But once back in New Zealand as a production, it was always running against budget (Ward and Maynard later had to forgo their fees to keep it afloat), logistical problems of location, and Ward's excessively self-absorbed habit of work. For example, the mountain lake sequences had to be shot in just two days by remote Lake Harris, high in the South Island's Alps, where the only access was by daily helicopter, and both cast and crew suffered from the excessive cold. Work in bitter weather in a disused quarry near Auckland Airport was finally brought to a halt by the crew holding an emergency meeting about general discontents and organisational inefficiencies. The three-storey cathedral spire set simply collapsed one day, smashing into a thousand pieces, with Ward having to shoot close-ups against remaining fragments of it to complete these sequences. The submarine sequences were shot in a former sewage pond, known to everyone as "bullshit lake", and crew members fell ill with hallucinations and vomiting. Even the second unit suffered disaster, in pursuit of the key shot of the falling torch; in a cavern over 300 feet underground, the cameraman's Arriflex plummeted into an underground river and imploded in its case. Virtually everyone succumbed to a 'flu virus, and eventually, bit by bit, the production began to wind apart, with both Maynard and Ward removing locations from the schedule in order to attempt to hold down costs; "his main worry was that the film might never be finished, mine that it might not be worth finishing", Ward later wrote. Ward accuses himself of developing a siege mentality towards the project.[9] Eventually, there was nothing left. "The final section was shot just ahead of the bulldozer tearing down the sets in an empty production shed, with one apple box, one actor, and a camera". It was a film, Ward remarks wryly, made "in lean times".

Premonition

The first image in the film is the moon, full, moving its elusive presence behind cloud, like a bacillus, a spore. It will be the race against the moon's setting which will eventually drive the story onwards, creating urgency and tension. Now, however, time is in suspension, tranced, and it is the boy Griffin (Hamish McFarlane) who is held in thrall, his mind presented with sudden, explosive fragments of escape, of elsewhere. Ward cleverly expresses the ambiguities of the moon's promise by mirroring its presence in the reflective surface of the lake, in which, it is gradually revealed, Griffin is standing. This visual device disorientates the point of view, allowing for both actual and imagined reflections to appear in the water, and then breaths of wind along its surface dislodging and dissolving the images held there. It is uncertain, even at this stage, if the swaying boy, his eyes constantly hovering between being wide-open and totally closed, is looking upwards or downwards. This emphasis on insecure verticalities, of laborious ascension and helpless fall, will become a central pivot of Ward's *mise en scène* throughout the film.

The montage of images which break into Griffin's semi-consciousness, warmed into colour by strong light and by flame, is a literal forewarning of those events which will become the body of the story. We are presented with the brief, startling evidences which will fuel Griffin's stubborn will, and provide markers for the journey of the pilgrims. We see the fierce violent work with the mining engine; the blue-black queen-fish breaking the surface of the water; the distant vision of the illuminated tower of the cathedral; the blindfolded Griffin walking quickly; hands reaching up on the rungs of a ladder; the tower standing stark upwards against a hurtling sky; Griffin's warning shout as he spies a figure nearing the top of the spire; the face of a pilgrim flattened by the terrible wind; the desperate circling climb up the stone spiral; the gloved hand slipping off the rung; the smallness of a rag of cloth (the gauntlet) falling through an infinity of sky; the silhouette of the cross being lifted into place; those same gloved hands pushing out across water what later is revealed to be a coffin. But, because all of these images, bright and dense as stained glass in a church window, are intercut with close-ups of Griffin plainly "seeing" them, Ward skilfully creates a deception in the viewer's mind, quite apart from the fact that they are not strictly in what will be revealed as the correct order. Griffin's passivity under the moon's hypnotic hold makes him seem merely an innocent witness to these possible events. The premonition hides his actual fate from him, and from us.[10]

This four-minute opening, quite clearly a prologue, also introduces us to the way in which the soundtrack is used throughout the film. There is a consistent oscillation between a spare, bare plateau of the natural wind and water sounds which surround Griffin in the lake, and a richly intimate mosaic of voices and instruments which are beginning to enunciate the themes of religious awe and epic quest. Percussive blows on both drums and bells constantly alert us to the immanence of this. And a further exaggerated and orchestrated natural sound energises both image and theme: the sound of flame suddenly brought and passed in front of the ear, which characterises the heat of human will, desire and invention, excited in the way that burning flame is, hot with passion and discovery, plunging itself again and again into the crevasses of the unknown, lighting the way with a human urgency, in absolute contrast to the still and implacable moon.

Vision and revelation

Vision is different from the purely visual. The visual is obviously a central component of any film; we are invited to gaze on surfaces and appearances, and, in every act of such looking, there is an expectation of meaning. The word "vision" on the other hand reminds us how the correlation within image sequences can "apprehend" a reality outside and beyond that accessible to language and reason. Ward's meticulous pursuit of visual acuity (matched by a similarly precise approach to the aural dimension) creates for the viewer a heightened reminder of the possibility, in the secular sense provided by photography, of revelation. In *Another Way of Telling* (1982), a book which deals primarily with still photography, John Berger reminds us that:

> Revelation was a visual category before it was a religious one. The hope of revelation - and this is particularly obvious in every childhood - is the stimulus to the *will* to all looking which does not have a precise functional aim.[11]

It goes without saying that looking at any film assumes a visual acuity beyond the precisely functional. However, most feature films are shot with a presumption that their visualisation affords the viewer a more functional access to other, more important considerations - most obviously, narrative, story and character. In suggesting that appearances might well constitute, in themselves, a "half-language", Berger stresses that our expectation of revelation, "when what we see does surpass us", is more frequent than we might suspect.

Furthermore, and most interestingly in relation to Ward's films, Berger reminds us that appearances, prior to the logical-positivist revolutions which stressed measurement and difference, rather than visual correspondence as the most vital components of human perception, were treated in all cultures as signs, as legend. The legendary is literally "that which is there to be read". Religious and magical beliefs hold that the visible is nothing but a coded message, and whatever our subsequent historical explanations about appearances – and scientific revolution in the modern sense is always posited on one version or another of the premise "there's more to this than meets the eye" – nevertheless their enigma remains. As Berger says: "Philosophically, we can evade the enigma. But we cannot *look* away from it."[12]

Ward's films abound with intoxicated sight, and the stories which elaborate themselves around it are themselves thematically and narratively defined in terms of seeing, vision and revelation. The very titles *Vigil*, *The Navigator* and *Map of the Human Heart* suggest particular ways of tackling the inscrutability of appearances. It is not the place of this study to look more broadly at Ward's work as a director, but this is an aspect which needs to be stressed. In *Vigil*, Toss' devotional watchfulness over the memory of her dead father gives the familiar surfaces of her world an intensity and an explosiveness which in some mysterious way guarantee the integrity, the perpetuation of her love for him. It goes without saying, of course, and recalling Berger's remarks on childhood's tireless readiness for revelation, that the protagonists of both this film and *The Navigator*, the provocateurs of the images offered to us on the screen, are children, little criminals of perception; and this childlike and "savage" sensibility is also carried forward through the central character of Avik, the Inuit "Holy Boy" of *Map of the Human Heart*.[13]

Crisis

Following the enigma of incoherent visions, in *The Navigator* we are suddenly shifted to clear-eyed topography, achieved by that most artful of pull-back shots – the snowball in the face. Suddenly, it is daytime – itself a rare commodity in this film – and the children of the community are mocking Griffin's absurd immobility in the lake. Connor's wife Linnet (Sarah Peirse) scolds him with the information that this is the fourth time this week that he has been up to these peculiar tricks. "Get out of the water!" Having hooked our attention with a dramatic and impressionistic collage of images and sounds, the following fifteen minutes of the film, through eight distinct sequences, are crammed with careful detail and exposition on the time, place and circumstance of Griffin's village.[14] The exotically remote location is finely tuned by a host of devices: the quaintly elaborate diction and dialect of the inhabitants; the bare, snow-covered landscape, and the way it has to be countered in terms of light and heat, shelter and clothing; the routines of the working day within this primitive ore-mining and smelting settlement; the vigorous life of rumour and superstition running through a simple and illiterate culture; the sets of relationships between families and generations; and the grim fight for survival against both the known and the unknown. But these rich descriptive tapestries are not indulged in for their own sake; they are all serving the basic narrative drive, which is to bring the situation in the village to crisis point.

Initially, as the day develops, we are shown what is familiar to Griffin; firstly, the house in which he lives, the anxiety about the absent Connor (Bruce Lyons), the central presence of chirpy grandmother (Kathleen-Elizabeth Kelly), and morose grandfather (Roy Wesney) leaning over with a piece of pragmatic advice which he presumably delivers most days: "Dreamers will be clothed in rags, Griffin!". The camera cranes after the boy as he climbs through the village, sharing once again shy glances with the little blonde girl who is looking after the chickens, finding once again his "uncles" with whom he spends many working days, the brothers Searle (Marshall Napier) and Ulf. On this day, the routine is slightly altered. The two men are raising a simple spiked cross to the roof of their house, one on which fortune has never been particularly kind, as protection against the plague. The banter between the three of them is quick and warm, nevertheless, for this community is one extended family, and people, kith or kin, young or old, are used to sharing burdens and long hours together. Eventually, the vastness of the terrain opens up before us in all its wintry glory as the three of them are joined by a fourth, Martin (Paul Livingston). It is only now, at the end of this continuous movement through a host of details out to a breathtaking panorama, that a caption quietly informs us of the time and place: "Cumbria March 1348".

Antipodean[15]

A quick initial close-up has introduced each of these three uncles. All three will go on the subsequent pilgrimage, and Ward, together with his screenwriters Kely Lyons and Geoff Chapple, will develop them within the story as main characters, whose different temperaments will illuminate the theme of simple, honest and unsophisticated men forced to grapple with a scale of events conjured to test their powers of faith and endurance. In a sense, the religious pilgrimages or crusades, innumerable journeys which we associate with the Christian Middle Ages, act as precursors to the later European voyages of discovery, pillage and colonisation. Together with the parallel developments in scientific understanding and technology, a fragmented peasant folk transformed itself into a confident and rapacious nationality, then Empire. Part of the dialectic intention of Ward's film is to image the opposing, as it were, temporal poles of this geographic and technical evolution within Western culture, in order to trace, with a sense of moral conscience, the implications of a "navigation" of the world driven by blind faith and appalling diet, to one, perhaps penultimately, based on social discipline, atomic power and satellite guidance.

Although the main characters in the film are drawn in intimate and quirky detail, they also represent archetypes of our voyaging progenitors. Searle is physically the strongest, possibly the oldest, and certainly a man not unfamiliar with responsibility and leadership. But there is something about him which lacks subtlety and flexibility, which is literally surly, as well as suspicious, and easily deflected or frightened. He is a man who needs the constant reassurances of the familiar, who can be thoroughly disorientated within a few steps west of the well-trodden, and who can panic and thrash out. Ulf, on the other hand, is humility and gentleness personified. He is simple, even simple-minded, a child in a gargantuan body, a creature of grunts and smiles rather than words, and, when he does speak at any length, his conversation is most typically with the inanimate and the invisible. Only approximately can he keep himself within the orbit of adult behaviour, his gyroscope is so easily knocked a-kilter. He is always coming along behind, a willing packhorse, often berated by the others, particularly Searle, and yet he carries within himself great dignity, and we are made to feel that the emotional life which inhabits the mountainside of his flesh is worthy of infinite respect, as something deeply human and untranslatable. Beside him, Martin is hardly corporeal at all, mostly nervous energy, sharp-eyed as the bird which is his namesake, sensitive to the moment and its immediate issues. Intelligent and articulate, his role is as arbiter and conscience, and, in a time when Reason has hardly come to be invented, he is its spokesman. Given access to books and learning, he might have proved to be an intellectual, or, at least, a fine shop steward.

Respectful of others, he is their good friend, reliable to the last, with a keen heart. He is aware that circumstances can change, and that such changes have significances that might be measured, and in time found useful. These three will be joined in due course by the pragmatic Arno (Chris Haywood), his curly blond hair flared out by the winter's winds, physically willing despite his missing hand. These are men whose knowledge of the world is more in their strong limbs than in their active heads; artisans, labourers, the salt of the earth, whose consciousnesses are restricted by the broadness of their ignorance and the desperateness of their faith. It says much for all four of them, these eventual voyagers who have never before left their native village, that, in their collective naïvety and helplessness, they will so willingly place their destiny in the hands of a demented boy.

The camera captures in a few bold strokes what makes up most of the days for these companions. They greet Chrissie (Charles Walker), the old man at the top of the mining shaft (a version of the mythic gatekeeper), and his windlass lowers them into the caves and tunnels which they and their ancestors have hacked out of the rock. Although, in this sequence, we do not see them at work, the later descent into the bowels of the earth – a combination of limb-wrenching labour and paltry, inexact technology, smothering in a confusion of dust and smoke and water, a rage of brute force against matter – offers us graphic illustration of the tasks of such early industry. Violent body heat followed by the numbing cold of the passageways, illuminated by the barest of naked flames, each man always within hailing distance of the next, in case of rockfall or worse – these are the repetitions which frame a few moments rest and reflection together. Griffin's notching into a stick the accumulating days of his brother's absence marks also the eternal tedium of his own incarceration. But, on this particular day, a series of shouts break the monotony.

Ward's wonderful cinematic vigour explodes into life around this moment; Griffin hurrying to the bottom of the shaft, the whoosh of flames, the others climbing into the basket, the whole thing heavily and slowly swaying upwards through different levels of the workings, convivial and claustrophobic, hands reaching and voices crying out in celebration the name of "Connor!". On the surface, the returned brother is first seen only in the distance, a waving figure, but we move closer to him, first with the approaching Griffin, culminating in the warmth of their embrace ("Look at them; you'd think they were married", observe the approving threesome, for the moment a comedy trio, from the top of the shaft), and then through a series of reacknowledgments of ties on Connor's part, primarily with Linnet, who offers a quick digest of the most urgent news, but then to the three men, and ultimately to the entire village. "So strange to see people smiling", muses the returned traveller.

Connor will eventually be the sixth pilgrim. He is different to the others, most obviously because he has already betrayed the restlessness, the sense of dissatisfaction, which marks out the archetypal hero. It is never explained why he needed to leave the village, but, as soon as we see him, his finely chiselled features, his dark searching eyes, we are aware of the sensibility of a man who, unlike those to whom we have already been introduced, could never be confined within the narrow boundaries of this village life. Whatever his need to have travelled, the narrative alerts us to a certain impulsiveness; after all, this is a man who has quit his home while his wife is in the latter stages of what appears to be a first pregnancy. While warmed and gratified by the welcome offered by the village, and glad to see familiar faces, there is something elusive about his smile, something not to be trusted, something that suggests he is already wanting to be off again. Ward marks this beautifully in a measured beat: with Griffin still in his embrace, and the boy's words, "You won't go away like that no more, Con - will you?", in his ears, Connor's gaze moves inexorably away from the moment, full of regret and longing, into himself, and the need for a life marking its own mysterious passage for itself, and not heedlessly sacrificed to the community. Connor expresses as much to Griffin a moment or two later, when he presents him with the beads made from hawthorn - "A scraggy tree, small and tough. It reminded me of someone". His own soul is made of the same material, but the image he draws of himself touches on a different dimension; "It's the tree they make axles from, Griffin. Axlewood". And with this breath comes a subconscious identification with the movement, into time and space, generated by such a primal technology: "If I'm the big wheel on the move...". We have already seen the big wheel of Chrissie's primitive windlass to get a sense of its role in dislodging the materials for the world's industrialisation, and, of course, later we will see Connor pinned to the terrifying, accelerating wheel of the Machine's history, in the shape of the locomotive which flashes by the oared boat and the unsaddled horse in the race to the cathedral. However, Connor's sentence has yet to reach its completion, and, when it does, it expresses the tragic dilemma of all heroes: "If I'm the big wheel on the move, still it's you at my heart...", he says to Griffin. "You and Linnet". He feels himself bound by something that, in truth, can never bind him. Perhaps when he is away he wishes only to be home; but home can never keep him. When Linnet arrives, effusive with her love and gratitude at his return, she seems immediately to be inhabiting a smaller universe than he. She is his dutiful and caring wife, but not his soul mate. As we will later find out, he is already infected by something, he already carries within him a knowledge greater than his ability to comprehend it. In fact, the only way in which he can verbally express it is through the words which describe evidences for the world's corruption, the torment created by the advance of the plague. If he is putting something over on the others, he is also incapable of not putting it over on himself; his name, after all, is the closest the film offers to the definition of a type. The conner is the person who activates the con, the wilful deception. The root gives growth in the English language to a whole host of definitions which struggle with the idea of knowledge, conscious or unconscious, deliberately manœuvred or helplessly acquired. And it would not be entirely inappropriate to remember that, in the technology which Ward later chooses to foreground as a lethal component of Western consciousness, the conning tower is the single most obvious detail of a submarine's architecture, and the one, in the film, which challenges the pilgrim's own vulnerable craft. It is the fate of the tragic hero that he does not know what it is that he is doing, or why. His "con" of steering the mission to success is that he knows such success also implies a doom, but one which he cannot acknowledge. Even as Connor smiles back to the welcome of his own folk, he carries the plague within him.[16]

Plague

Martin's initiative in creating an emergency village council brings issues to a head. "Do we panic or do we plan?", he asks them. In the thematic territory explored by *The Navigator*, what we are dealing with turns out to be a profoundly significant example of Free Will's struggle with Fatalism's inertia. History is pitted with such moments, but few which rape the ontological with such savagery. The Pestilence, or Great Mortality, as those times emphatically nominated it, poured itself upon populations with a disregard that beggared any belief. It was a malevolence that possessed neither rhyme nor reason. Beyond the abstract approximations of astrology, no direct cause or precise location could be given to it. In just retribution to the iniquity and corruption of humankind, God's wrath in all its absoluteness had been finally roused. Travelling west at an almost measurable speed, in two short years the Pestilence removed a third of the human population between India and Ireland. The fact that its virulence accommodated itself in the stomach of the flea, and the bloodstream of the rat which was the flea's host, was beyond any framework of understanding available at the time (indeed, it would be fully 500 more years before a bacillus would present itself to human view). But the immediacy of its impact very quickly provided overwhelming evidence to anyone surviving such events that the end of the world was surely at hand. No matter who you were or what you did, Doom was standing at the corner of your neighbour's house, riding by with the spring rains, or filling itself up into the belly of the waxing moon. Barbara W Tuchman's observations on the aftermath of the catastrophe, however, also suggest the devastation to be a significant contributor to the evolution of a historically modern European sensibility:

> Survivors of the plague, finding themselves neither destroyed nor improved, could discover no Divine purpose in the pain they had suffered. God's purposes were usually mysterious, but this scourge had been too terrible to be accepted without questioning. If a disaster of such magnitude, the most lethal ever known, was a mere wanton act of God or perhaps not God's work at all, then the absolutes of a fixed order were loosed from their moorings. Minds that opened to admit these questions could never again be shut. Once people envisioned the possibility of change in a fixed order, the end of an age of submission came in sight; the turn to individual conscience lay ahead. To that extent the Black Death may have been the unrecognized beginning of modern man.[17]

Between the opposite poles of *The Navigator*'s narrative, two civilisations antipodean to each other, but joined by a mutual umbilical cord brutally driven via the centre of the earth, runs the idea of ontological doubt, personified by two brothers, one in open childish glee, the other in cowled shadow, whose intimate connectivity traces the historical struggle to navigate towards a world not cowed by death. Historical determinism enters the frame of Western thought. As Tuchman concludes: "An event of great agony is bearable only in the belief that it will bring about a better world".[18]

Martin's question, "Do we panic or do we plan?", elicits only confused fragments of response. Cold night has fallen again – and the film will inhabit the various shades of night and darkness from now until the pilgrims' return the following dawn, stretching Ward's and his director of photography Geoffrey Simpson's powers of invention for light sourcing and keying.[19] In this scene on the smelting ground, the flames of torches furl and flutter, as the shreds of evidence and rumour which have been accumulating through the several previous scenes coalesce. Arno is convinced that an offering should be taken to the distant cathedral he has heard is being built to the west. Connor remains apart. Searle is adamant about sitting tight. Plainly, he has little support from the villagers, who respond strongly to the Celtic cross which Chrissie holds before them. Martin optimistically assumes that Connor will be the first to support the idea of a pilgrimage to save the settlement, but, when finally provoked to speak, Connor's cruel experience of his travels has convinced him that no action will prevail: "We've got a month, maybe two". Despite Chrissie and Martin's encouragement, both possible leaders for a journey in search of salvation are playing possum.

The deadlock is broken by shouts of "Looters!". The community is already being invaded. The night is filled with cries. A drum beats, men run into and out of the swirling light. The camera swoops up suddenly over a rise, to reveal close to the shore of the lake an organised line of people with long staves repelling a crowded boat. As the main figures in the story arrive to see, we observe through their eyes the unfolding action, one which the villagers have plainly expected and rehearsed, reminding us yet again of the brutality of survival on these cold, barren uplands. But Connor and Martin are quick to see that this is no raiding party. "There's women and children on board...". As flaming arrows catch the limp sail alight, we see the chaos on board illuminated – bewildered children, desperate men trying to douse the fire, a woman standing panicked, breathless with fear. We are aware of struggle, of people falling into the water.[20] The incident comes to a cruel, indecisive conclusion. The fat moon, the plague's sign, hangs overhead, as the villagers, almost in trance, stare at the boat, now bereft of life, burning listlessly out in mid-lake, the fate of its passengers unknown. As a narrative device, this action sequence has upped the stakes, brought home to the villagers the likely fate of their own families should they be once uprooted by panic and forced to flee. They have now seen the evidence of the plague's advance with their own eyes.

The need for quest

In the night's idle hours, warily on guard, two ideas have grown in the minds of the men: escape and expiation. Escape is the purely practical solution to the problem, but even the normally pragmatic Arno can only grasp at straws:

> I heard a story once. About them old pits up behind the mine. They reckon there's a... there's a hole up there so deep if you dropped a stone down it, sooner or later it'd fall out the far side of the earth.

Appropriately, it is Martin who is tackling the more complex task of atonement, an action the essence of which is to reconcile or restore friendly relations between God and sinners. The villagers have already begun to debate that founding and most fundamental idea within human culture, of averting disaster by the performance of rites or ceremonies. However, there is no great evidence offered in the film of a highly elaborated or established religious environment; these are marginal people, scraping a bare survival by their wits and inventiveness, creating a proto-industrial community, not an obviously agricultural one, the sort in which, at a later historical date, religious nonconformity might find its natural home. Their faith is something born of the sweat of their skin, the ache of their limbs, the silence of the moor.[21] But they do have a notion of a centre (the cathedral), and hold fast to the power of Christianity's symbols. The two ideas, of a practical escape from disaster, and yet a feeling of total helplessness which can only be responded to by an act of atonement, are meshed, in the instant, by Griffin's first mention to them of his dream.

The predicament of the village having been ratcheted up to breaking-point, the next few sections propel us rapidly into decisive action, orchestrated with great skill, and built up through the differing psychologies of the characters we have begun to know. In a beautiful verbal image, Connor expresses the depths of his own current despair and sense of helplessness in the face of the evidence they have all witnessed: "It's the full moon bears contagion for it like a sack. At sunrise, she lets it fall...on us!".

Griffin suddenly slumps to the ground as fragmented images of his dream reappear to him in startling colour. Searle's scepticism conveys the fact that he views the boy as merely suffering some unfortunate affliction, but Linnet, impelled perhaps by the need to find hope for the future of her soon-to-be-born child, passionately reminds them all that his premonitions have proved in the past to turn out true. It is this moment that tips the balance; Connor suddenly accedes, "It's our only chance". Martin is delighted. Arno and Ulf are already committed. Connor is adamant that Griffin will come with them. Searle is more bewildered than opposed; "You're all daft!". But the flame has been lit. We follow it as the camera pans a landscape of many accumulating torches, to the steady beat of a drum, and the journeying, wordless hymn of male voices begins to define the narrative as epic.

In a film without any significant female presence, the character of Ulf conveys both a certain vulnerability of the flesh and an openness to emotion as traits of a particular compassion for life. Very much, one feels, his mother's son, we find him in front of the wooden cross of her grave, dedicating the forthcoming pilgrimage to her memory, assuring her that the one thing of value they possess, a small icon of the Virgin Mary, will find a proper home, a blessed home, in the cathedral they will seek and find. Whereas these smelters and smiths will seek to hoist through sheer will and brute strength the heavy barbed spike to the highest and most visible point, as a challenge accepted and a great danger overcome, Ulf's modest project will hardly be noticed by anyone. This brief moment of intimacy ends with a tender kiss for the cross. He is prodded back out into the open by an irate Searle, who complains how rolling, shambling Ulf can never be relied on, even at moments as important as this: "always too far in front, or too far behind". So now, all in a line, the pilgrims pass, and the camera cranes up and round to see them on their way.

Black-and-white and colour[22]

Ward's skilful use of colour and monochrome is one in which narrativity, thematics and iconography are bound together with a sense of the "poetics" of the medium, as we will find, for example, in films such as Andrej Tarkovskij's *Andrej Rublëv* (1966) or Wim Wenders' *Wings of Desire* (1986).[23] On a purely schematic level, the temporality underpinning the narrative is that which is shown in black-and-white. The events which are the products of Griffin's dream, or vision, are those depicted in colour. And this demarcation is clearly adhered to throughout the film. However, it is problematised within the narrative by the fact that, as Griffin recounts to the others step-by-step, the details of his original vision (the one experienced, presumably, during the opening sequence where he is standing in the icy lake), they themselves begin to participate as protagonists within the vision. They become agents making the individual vision a collective reality, which we, as audience, experience as the reality of the ongoing narrative. In other words, we do not simply regard the narrative as an unfolding depiction of Griffin's vision alone (in which he dreams that the others are taking part), but rather as an adventure shared by the living participants within it. The premise of the film, in fact, depends on Griffin being able to search out the original vision with the physical help of the others, and, as we shall see, the dreamer can be blind to the details of his own dream, just as the other protagonists within it are free to subvert and transform the direction of the dream by their own exertions. Even though the eventual outcome will be fatal to himself, the visionary provides the others with the "will" or the "blessing", depending on one's ontological point of view, to survive. As the physical adventure of the group, guided by Griffin, directs them "into the future", then we have to see the colour sequences within the film as illustrating in some way an evolutionary thematic within human endeavour, one based upon a subtle combination of technological inventiveness and religious conviction, a drive towards an end, perhaps a kind of precursor to the inductive reasoning which underlies the Western scientific, result-producing view of the world. The use of black-and-white within the film, on the other hand, represents the weight, the pain, the thrall of the immediate present, within which any individual human life span is enslaved, upon which fate, chance and doom can play their tricks. Only by entertaining a sense of (impossible) possibility, driven perhaps by desperation, building itself into a collective pursuit (a quest), does what we call culture, a mixture of apprehension, emotion and ingenuity, grow. Only within the adventure of Time can humanity survive.

Engine

This whole issue is foregrounded by the presence of the mining engine. In the momentary hiatus Ward creates as the men find themselves suddenly underground and facing the odds, Griffin forcefully puts the case for technological momentum:

> We're tunnelling through the earth, all of us, and we're using an engine. The engine's got a shaft, for breaking the rock and dirt. It's the engine, you see, that makes us go fast enough to be there before the moon turns full.

It is well to remember that the root of the word "engine" lies in the Latin "ingenium", referring more to particular human dispositions than to objectivised machinery, but, as its etymology hardens through English by way of genius, ingenuity, artfulness, trickery, contrivance and appliance, a definition eventually comes to rest most precisely upon that of a device which possesses the means of generating power, whether this be caloric, gaseous, electrical or, ultimately, nucleic. It would overstate the obvious to recall that the canons of Western knowledge and expertise have been largely created by a great variety of engineers. And, of course, as an expression of collective human power, power over nature, power to "tunnel through" and transform the earth, power of human groups over others, this latter finds an eventual realisation in the power of nationality and in the nation state. Significantly, it is Martin, the rationaliser, who first comes upon the machine itself, lying apparently derelict next to the huge fissure that Arno had previously mentioned. But we are still within the film's monochrome regime. The device is "really" here, in the present, even though plainly none of the men, to judge by their awed silence, has ever set eyes on, let alone imagined, it before. But neither does the device belong solely to Griffin's personal vision ("I've never been down here before", he protests to Connor), even though he has anticipated it, and recognises what must be done with it once discovered. How has it come to be here?

Obviously someone has left it here, from the past – ancestors of the present crew, perhaps; or, more likely, since it would seem to be a matter of generations, rather than centuries, since it was constructed – and because this early mining represents a way of life which is brief and opportunistic, rather than possessing agriculture's more conservative set of consistencies – a previous community with no connection at all to this present one, other men at another time, so there was never any specific memory of such machinery to be transmitted. The engine was created one time, perhaps unavailingly employed, and then forgotten – although the rumour of the great abyss, at the same time, had remained in currency. The earth of human civilisations is full of such decaying relics, some of which point to constantly evolving lines, some to evolutionary dead ends.[24] The miners have stumbled upon this machine by a kind of "hallowed" chance, led there by the feverish delusions of a boy, but once there, they are in a position to recognise what could be achieved with such a device, because, whatever their individual doubts and bewilderments, collectively they are familiar with the idea and labour of mining, and because they have a profound collective necessity at this moment in time; they have been driven here by a catastrophe, and survival demands that they take certain steps, immediately, instinctively and without thought. What Griffin is driven by is a deadly certainty, the perverse mystery of intemperate imagination, which all cultures have always seen as being closely allied to sickness and madness. But the group needs his madness because the world itself is in the grip of madness, and they are slowly allowing themselves to be swayed by it.[25]

Griffin allows them not a moment for thought or doubt. He hurls his flaming brand into the void, upon the edge of which the men sway in collective terror, inviting them to suicidal risk, illuminating the path which they must follow. Here the torch falls, both in close-up and wide shot of emphatic black-and-white, inviting the eyes and the ears of the men to contemplate the sheer distance with which they will have to engage, the reality of it, step-by-step. Ward has used the image of the vertical pit and the falling torch a number of times in the film, both in monochrome and in colour, as a reiterative device, expressive of both a subjective and an objective reality, a powerful and ambiguous symbol of human intelligence, at once the single flame (of heat and light) stolen by Prometheus from Olympus, and from which all human power over the world originated, as well as evoking Lucifer's prideful expulsion from the heavens, as Lord of Chaos and rebel against all preordained authority, exponent of the dangers and devices of free will within the helplessness of free fall, ever and onwards. But here it points to an absolute and specific moment, the one in which Griffin says, "We follow the torch...we use the machine to tunnel".

Thresholds and maps

With a sudden cut, a crash of sound and explosion of sudden light and colour, the men are at work, the engine has been put to task, and, with a splendid phallic energy, the material of the earth is being penetrated – an anticipation of the explosive "kick" which can be delivered by a later manifestation of this very same engine, the nuclear submarine and its warheaded missiles.[26] It is a good, dramatic cut, sublime[27] in the sense that an editing moment which is sudden and decisive excites our pleasure in being spectators. The labour is being observed with an almost documentary precision to the steady working beat of a drum, interrupted and contextualised from time to time, and these brief breaks serve to weave greater complexity around the repetitive action. Firstly, the camera pulls out to locate the obliquely descending path of the tunnel within the massive weight of rock, the smoky yellow flames dwindling into insignificance at the bottom of the frame. The pull-back is continued shortly afterwards, in an exquisite composite shot[28] to reduce the human figures to near invisibility beneath a layered vertical map of the journey, the surface of the earth, the lake and the settlement upon it, and the moon riding through clouds high above all. There is a simple, schematic quality to this map, its orientation recalling the demarcation of the Christian cosmos into the three vertically related levels of Heaven above, Earth between, and Hell below; a map drawn more by spiritual conviction than from empirical knowledge, and one within which the scale is still neighbourly, localised, within which human beings can be placed. The sound-mix in this shot shows how carefully Ward composes textual elements, the beat of human effort suddenly lost in the cold voice of winds suspended between trumpet notes, penetrated by a sundering thundercrack.

Separating these two visual interpolations, heralded by an open-throated cry and sharp, thin notes blown on a trumpet, in the patch of sky still visible up the shaft within which the fat moon squats, flies the emblematic figure of Death, a skeleton in a ragged cloak, with a steady beat of smothering wings. What is interesting here is the figure's perfect artificiality as an emblem, a shadow puppet cast and mechanically mobile against the moon's glare, despite the fact that the shot is in black-and-white, which conventionally has been used to define the documentary present. A fantastic projection of the men's fear, it nevertheless draws eye-boggling and breath-catching reaction from Arno, although from the "dream-delivering" side of the colour narrative; a man reacting in his dream to something he is seeing in reality (although it palpably is not real!), which is a complete reversal of any filmic convention. A moment or two later, the final return to monochrome is in a brief sequence which, ambivalently, could either be a flashback or a flashforward. The group is standing, again uncertainly on the brink, and the subject again is the impossibility of the journey. Ulf's pleading voice seems to suggest that the journey has never begun, and possibly never can begin:

> But, Griffin, you'd fall straight through to the other side
> of the earth after just two days' digging. Into the sky! Or
> you'd have to cling like a tick.

Griffin's reply, couched in the past tense, which implies that (of course, for him in his vision, but also for all of them) the journey is already a thing of the past, fully achieved and being remembered, for all its danger and difficulty: "It was further than we'd thought. Three times the length of your rope, Arno – no...all of six times that length, before we struck the last hard rock between us...and the far side of the world...".

Immediately the film plunges back into the frenzy of tunnelling, to the single, newly-established time-line and the now-total employment of colour (into the sublimated text, in other words), and through the penetrating of the next "threshold", into the historical present, or what the script calls "The New World". It is important to mark this point, however, as the one which leaves open the question to what degree the men "really" make the journey to their eventual destination, a problem which is central to the display of the thematic concerns of the film outlined above.

Two further "maps" await the travellers, once they have pierced the wall between Then and Now, a moment in which we see the delivery of the engine's final blow from one side, and the thrust of the bolt through collapsing masonry at the other. To these subsistence villagers, the two maps provide different views of the (mythic) magnitude of the City. "Whatever city is up there must be... vast", whispers Martin, the weight of the future suddenly hanging over their heads.[29] Down has suddenly become Up (although Ulf is still worried that this might not be the case, and that they will all tumble away eternally into the void), and Up will shortly become Out. The first map is a maze of tunnelled structures, which Connor, the travelled one, recognises as the city's sewers, where the air might be poisonous or "full of contagion".[30] Although these sewers will, in the event, prove to be curiously unused and dry, the script thoughtfully and briefly provides a primitive device for tackling Connor's fear, the "air-bladder" (an actual pig's bladder – nature directly engineering culture)[31] which presumably all the men have about them as marginal protection against the foul air of underground, and which Connor reminds Griffin to use, as he is about to set forth, Arno's rope acting as umbilical cord. For the first time, Connor utters the familiar but ambiguous (given what we later come to know of his character and Luciferian role) "Godspeed", a conjunction within a single word of the very thematic thrust of the narrative, faith accelerating itself into a new dimension.

This short passageway is traversed in the conventional terms of narrative film tension: a musical build, intercutting between Griffin's puff-cheeked progress, the slowly unwinding rope through Connor's gauntleted hands, his unavailing calls to the boy, and the apprehensive faces of the waiting men. Two distinctive colour tones define the intervening distance of the sewer; the soft, dust-suffused yellow of the torches reminding us of where the men have come from, and the sharp, cold white light, tinged with blue, of the down-beaming night sky, anticipating the street lights of the city, to where they are headed. Griffin's distant shouts of arrival transform their anxiety into jubilation, and they begin to move; only Ulf's hesitancy and tear-stained face holds their advance, marking the emotional transition which is occurring to them: "I'm afraid", he sobs to the passing Searle. Significantly, it is Ulf's face which Ward chooses to frame as our initial guide to the new world, his eyes wide, his mouth broadening into an almost mischievous grin. This third map heralds itself with a blast of full orchestra; a slow right-to-left pan across a territory defined only in lights, an amalgam of St Augustine's City of God[32] and the science-fiction city in which matter has transformed itself into pure energy. The group stands looking down from an exposed hillside, and the face of each man punctuates the pan, the light in his eyes reflecting the awe he might feel for both possibilities, although, appropriately, it is Martin who is already testing out the logistics of it all: "Think how much tallow you'd need for all that!". These three maps have traced a sense of the world in which a verticality has moved itself towards a horizontality.[33] The threshold of time has been crossed. "That's the city. The one I've been seeing in my dreams!", shouts Griffin. Now they can all see it.

For Martin, the journey has already provided palpable evidence which is extending his grasp, his optimistic temperament and open, dialectic-embracing mind allowing him to interpret it entirely positively:

> Lights...water...trees...grass, and...something sticks it all to earth. God's goodness! It makes sense! Anything flat's got two sides, and if the evil was our side, then surely God's goodness is...

The worry is that, despite arrival, not everything is as expected. The vista before them provides no sight of the great church, and this triggers Searle's doubt. One feels the human qualities in this man, his courage, fear, obstinacy and integrity, the rock around which others can jump and squeal; it is his sense of protection and proportion which contributes to survival just as much as the risk-taking of Connor and Griffin, or the fancies of Martin, the helpless affection of Ulf, the reliable fraternity of Arno. Searle is the shepherd dog, always at the rear, keeping check, taking count. He is the defender, the insistent proponent, of common sense. All the others have unquestioningly thrown themselves in with the boy's convictions and predictions, but when even Griffin shows uncertainty when faced with the presence of Ulf's wooden virgin ("I'm sure I'll keep remembering things as we go along, you know"), it is Searle's face on which the camera lingers; the adventure is a kind of insanity, and he is the one, despite everything, who must remain sane. He will be severely tested in the next few minutes.

The threat of momentum

Ulf has rolled himself downhill, and is the first to encounter the barrier of the motorway which encircles this modern city. At first, we see the tranced pleasure in his face at the moving lights, and his repeated "So pretty" is underscored by the gentle harmonics of church music. The movement of light again plays a key role in this sequence, the flared yellow of the flames contrasting with the framed whiteness of car headlights, both grounded within the intense azure which, in this realm, characterises moonlight.

But suddenly the moving vehicles are real; they invade Ulf's space, they spin him around. We hear their sound, their horns, the squeal of their tyres. The others have pursued Ulf to the edge of the road, and their fearful shouts behind him add to his confusion. The camera is now alongside his predicament, wobbling precariously. Ulf's panic accelerates; he is being hunted, a huge ten-wheeler coming up behind. He drops the Virgin. His girth and his packs make it difficult for him to bend, as traffic whips past his fingertips. For the first time we hear his sobbing, his head turning from side to side, totally disorientated. In what, from both Noel Appleby and the others, will become a beautifully comic choreography, a road dance, between gesticulating pedestrians and implacable, impersonal vehicles, Ward immediately establishes the vulnerability of these journeymen and their faith, in terms of *speed*.[34] Technological progress implies a momentum, which, however much the product of reason and inductive thought, nevertheless characterises itself in the world as something beyond the ability of the human anatomy. Bodies are not adequate; they will not move sufficiently quickly. By laying the image of mother and child down directly on the asphalt, in the path of the juggernaut, Ward astutely establishes a sense of the particular danger to humans of the contemporary world, intoxicated by its own relentless powers of acceleration.

It is an intoxication which has already, from somewhere else, infected Connor, who insists, despite this immediate and palpable barrier, that they move "as the crow flies". There is a wonderful shot now of the group charging the road, with their brave and enthusiastic torches. Everything in the sequence of the crossing is achieved through the physical performance of the actors, dodging, weaving, bobbing and spinning, aided by the quick editing of a multiplicity of angles, offered by both static and moving camera. Finally, the men career onto the grassy bank opposite, where an unlikely neon sign welcomes them with the information that "Dewar's Whisky Never Varies", only to find that even their concerted, merely human pathway has been altogether too quick for the panicked Ulf. He is clutching his Virgin again, but he is on the other side of the road. Connor's call across to him, "You're supposed to come with us!", is a complaint so often aimed at recalcitrant humanity by self-appointed leaders tied to undeviating trajectories. Searle rages, throws his flame at a vehicle; but even his bulk is bounced aside for its trouble. Ulf is like some kind of hedgehog (a creature ubiquitously incapable of crossing asphalt without serious damage), beyond words, his limbs attempting to describe his terror and anguish, his body pointing in all directions except forwards, in this instant expelled from the adventure, this soft maternal man, forced to hunker down, to await the returning heroes. The stages of his failure to cross have been accompanied throughout by the flat, plaintive drone from a chanter. While losing nothing in the serious tone of his narrative, Ward shows a mischievous humour in this sequence, something which is obliquely present throughout the entire film: cutting and cruel, but never patronising.

Hand in glove

In this new place, nevertheless, the same moon is in the sky, darkly shadowed. A fresh image asserts itself in big close-up; a gauntlet, fallen on the ground, picked up by Griffin, and given back to his brother. As Connor pulls it onto his hand, the brothers look into each other's face. A change has occurred. With the gloved hand alone in shot, Connor brushes the hair back off Griffin's brow, touches his cheek; a gesture of tenderness, but the framing of the glove, and perhaps something in Griffin's expression imply the separation which is now occurring between them, perceived as a necessity by the older brother, already apprehending the curse he will have to carry, the sacrifices he will be forced to make. The gloved hand is here symbolising endeavour, leadership and the pursuit of ends which will justify all means. The gauntlet is characteristically medieval, but it has come to convey a sense of challenge beyond the mere formalities of the chivalric. "Throwing down", "picking up" and "running" the gauntlet in the world's recent times might more accurately express the experience of entrepreneurial capitalism in cahoots with mechanical and industrial know-how. With more ambiguous, urgent emotion, and for the second time to Griffin, Connor softly speaks the word "Godspeed", before suddenly announcing to everyone: "We separate here". He barks out his orders and his strategy. Searle, already bruised, and bereft at the loss of Ulf, can barely contain his emotion. The moistness in each of the men's eyes betokens their different situations: Connor keen, driven now, while Searle is wounded, at a loss. Connor's advice to him (to search for a foundry to cast the cross), to follow your nose, gauge the wind and "steer a course", exemplifies the empirical approach, a kind of sixth sense, which initially allowed humankind to discover its world as a coherent field within time and space. It is as if, on this side of the divide, the "navigation" roles are being redefined. As the power of the original seer (Griffin) seems to be losing its authority, Connor takes up the role of commander and strategist, appointing Searle as a lieutenant, with authority within his own area of expertise (metalwork).

Griffin protests, and feels the weight of this new hierarchy. A blow from the gloved hand strikes him to the ground. His own hand falls on broken glass and is cut. The moment has a triple resonance. It signifies Connor's willingness to put the wider issue of cause and community ahead of that of blood kin.[35] Secondly, it establishes the gauntlet as a significant component of the later climactic drama. Thirdly, and very cunningly, it underscores as a physical wounding, the spilling of family blood, the fact that somewhere in the course of things the bacillus of plague transmits itself from Connor to Griffin. In the very act of extolling, with all urgency, the cause of the greater good ("Let everyone just do what they have to do"), Connor fatally wounds his brother, whose blood will stain his conscience long after the successful completion of the adventure. Already as if unable to bear the guilt, Connor sweeps impetuously away into the darkness, and it is left to Martin to attempt to patch up the boy's anxieties at being abandoned, offering that "however big the city, there's only one Church". Whereas the truth is, in modern history, a creation of men more in the breed of Connor than Martin, it is the city, holus-bolus, as a cultural fact, which will totally replace the Church.[36]

Us and Them

A pick-up, that icon for new worlds built upon notions of individualism, straight lines, monocultural economies and rampant engineering, is the means by which artisans of the present first encounter their predecessors from the past. Not surprisingly, this one is rogue, with a life of its own hardly in the control of "bloody Eric", and in its hoonish behaviour seems deliberately bent on assassinating Griffin; brute horsepower has little time for "the vision thing". As Smithy (Desmond Kelly), Tom (Bill Le Marquand) and Jay (Jay Lavea Laga'aia) poke their noses out of the industrial workshop which tomorrow will finally close its doors, they naturally assume that these apparitions standing before them are nothing more than the usual street-life, creating a ruckus.[37] The script sees the important connection to be made here as one of mutual recognition at the level of the journeyman, the artisan who, in Marx's classic depiction for modern times, hires out for wages the instinctive and inherited labouring skills of his mind and body. The medieval jack of all trades manufactures entirely for the benefit of his own immediate community, according to faith and necessity. Within the city, industrial processes allow for the manufacture of surplus, managed by capital, and, however long the connection, the worker comes to be engaged within the process as a hired specialist, whose livelihood is ultimately dependent on the machinations of supply and demand. The situation of the three contemporary workers exemplifies this situation. We sense their workshop as existing in the midst of a larger plant, which tomorrow will cease operation, and the three of them will, no doubt as the result of severe "rationalisations", enter redundancy or redeployment. It would not be too far wide of the mark to argue that mass unemployment, and with it the loss of artisanal skills, has always been the plague of industrialised cultures; the one around which, in the secular populations of cities, real anxieties about "survival" have spun, and one brought to a particular kind of head in the late-20th century. Like every other country in the Western world, from the 1980s onwards, a gradual deconstruction of state-owned primary production resources has characterised New Zealand economic life, together with the notions of collective ownership which underpinned their original expansions of scale, in the face of international corporate power. Indeed, the pace of these reforms, towards a total reliance on the lotteries of "market forces", has been greater in New Zealand than most, celebrated, as elsewhere, by a reactionary politics emboldened into radicalism, as an "economic miracle". Money rules, and the three workers make it plain that this conditions their working lives; even to the extent of the (coincidental) work on the cathedral cross having to be indefinitely postponed for lack of funds, a fact which is not credible to Martin. "The church, poor?!", he exclaims, which produces the wry retort, "Like any other business, eh? When they don't want what you're selling...". Whatever the virtues or otherwise of the expediencies of late capitalism, the men have developed a stance towards such ceaseless winds of change: a kind of philosophical detachment, which, in this film, contains a particularly New Zealand set of inflections – no wasted words, a laid-back attitude to see what the other bloke will do first, a good-natured suspicion, "Fresh off the boat, are you, boy?", a willingness to encourage mateship without having to give away too much yourself, "Can you understand these buggers?" – a postcolonial society with an egalitarian soul as a kind of homogenisation of what were once distinctive, passionate and localised communities, of the kind, in fact, exemplified by the Cumbrians. There is more than a little irony in the moment when Jay hands Arno his can of Steinlager, and Arno sprays it back over him, his single, underplayed word to the others, "Ale!", perhaps suggesting this traditional medium of conviviality to be a more aerated spirit than the reliable substance he is used to. These contemporary smiths are certainly cooler shadows of their impassioned forebears.[38]

It is to *The Navigator*'s considerable strength that this encounter allows a generous recognition to occur between such remote cultures, the medievals working "a kind of spell" over the contemporaries, providing them with an urgency and a necessity which their everyday labours have hitherto lacked. It is not directly said within the extant dialogue, but the ways in which the three men are captured by both the substance and the form of the medievals' task convey a spiritual dimension, and one not allied only to the obvious Christian connotations of the cross. It is the *making* of the cross which forges their common acquaintance.[39] The script and Geoffrey Simpson's camera foreground the industrial moment of forging copper so emphatically, climaxing in the wonderful sequence in which the molten metal dances its way, like a demented golden snake, from the crucible, through the trough, and into the mould of the spike, that we are left in no doubt as to Ward's linking of communality, process, faith and form, in which the Aesthetic is bound ineluctably to the Political. Light and heat bring out the enthusiasm, literally, in each face.[40] So when the issue arises of completing the work on the cathedral roof, Smithy only hesitantly reintroduces the issue of money, and it is a point that slips away under the certainty of Martin's protestation, "The copper is a tribute". A tribute to life, to struggle, to craft, a made thing which is offered across time, against time just as much as for God, as the essential human gift. The acceleration of technology and industrialisation into the modern era is paralleled by the growth of a collective amnesia about the human worth at the centre of endeavour, and it is a particular mark of Ward's romanticism that he views such an evolution as meat for moral argument.

The natural sympathy between these men of different times points towards a utopian vision. It could be argued, however, that the film misses the obvious trick of its own speculative storyline, in which two times zones will collide in mutual antagonism in order to provoke dystopian apprehensions, an approach much more in accord with our own end-of-century sensibilities, and a prevailing tone within the whole evolution of "science-fiction". Ward's film moves unrelentingly forwards as an affirmation of the mission of the medievals. The fact that the venture takes place largely through the night makes it reasonable that we do not encounter the crowded workaday rush, but it is hard to believe, given contemporary obsessions with security and surveillance, that the anarchic presence of this gang of displaced persons would not attract more attention than it does. The narrative here could have established a more various set of interfaces between the past and the present by denying such an unimpeded access to the cathedral, ones which frustrate the quest of each character sufficiently to illuminate differences between the single-focused pre-technological religious community, and the disparate, secular, atomised post-technological culture of the present, one showing threat or indifference towards its own ancestry.[41] The journey from vision to created reality demands more in the representation of the present than, in fact, is provided. The assertion of the visual/aural dimension in advance of the dramatic has already been outlined in relation to Ward's work, and this can reveal a certain blandness, a fear of confrontation and human complexity, an over-reliance on the iconic and the schematic, a giving over of the human richness of story to the allure of mere spectacle, a fact which comes even more to the fore in his subsequent films, *Map of the Human Heart* and, with unctuous sentimentality, *What Dreams May Come* (1998).

City of terrible night

So, despite the easy kinship formed between the two groups of workers across time, *The Navigator* subsequently eschews the human dimension, and, in a series of brilliantly realised set-pieces, provides an evocation of an alien landscape populated by monsters, in which everything except the illuminated profile of the gradually revealed cathedral seems terrifyingly out of scale. The sequence also defines the trauma of time, the terrible, unknowable gap between Then and Now, to which the only human response is an open-mouthed howl of anguish; the medievals become much more animal-like than we have hitherto seen them, rapidly losing purpose and dignity, although their will, perversely, remains.

Arno, Searle and Griffin have stolen both a powerful white horse and a rowing-boat, crammed the former into the latter, and set off across water. Their perception is that the horse will provide the essential draught power to operate a lifting winch on the cathedral roof, and the way in which the animal features in the sequence provide a mythic reminder of its central role in the evolution of land-based cultures.[42] They may only have borrowed the animal from an unsuspecting early morning recreational rider - whose brief, fist-shaking appearance on the foreshore again establishes a comic component to these muscular visions - but Arno is in no doubt about the horse's traditional worth - "If they take a hand for a horse, what the hell are they going to take for a horse and a boat...?" - and the cruel retribution which follows hot on the heels of stealing one. But, in the sequence, it is the horse's vulnerability which is stressed, its hooved feet removed from reliable earth, its power confined and frustrated, and insignificant in comparison to the behemoth or leviathan which is already marking the surface of the water, sliding its way towards them.

The pan-piped misadventures of the quartet in the boat are replaced by a deep foreboding, the rush of water, resonant percussion, the tumbling of a bell-buoy, a shrieking trumpet of apocalypse. "Evil. An omen!", curses Searle. The impressionistic visuals which began the sequence, a single keylight defining space and action entirely in terms of sudden chiaroscuro (a frame made up only of illuminated horse's breath or the halo of Arno's hair), intensify as the "queen-fish" surfaces, hissing and spraying water, its glistening skin and elevated dorsal towering overhead in terrifying proximity, something elemental, a transmogrification of the moon's cruel monochromatic blue light, moment by moment solidifying between air and water. Its effortless presence is marked by a shift to a brazenly militaristic march snapped out on snare drum and pipe, and the brutal impenetrable steel of its flanks can be gauged by the ineffectual missiles hurled by Griffin and the oar wielded against it by Arno. In its imperturbability it has no intention to destroy them, although its passing exposes them, draining them of self-conviction. Griffin is held in a trance of terror, flooded by sequences of urgent images – all the party running into the cathedral; Connor *in extremis*; a gauntleted hand slipping its hold on a rung; a minute figure falling through immense sky; the shining cross slipping away below water; a coffin being thrust out over water – which are driving him to the core of truth which lies within his sense of premonition: "One of us will fall. One of us...dead." Searle's mood is black, self-pitying, with self-preservation his only thought. In probably the longest sustained speech of the film, the absoluteness of fate appals him:

> It's me, isn't it? The end for me. I've watched them all picked away. My wife in childbirth. The child she died for, picked away. My mother...picked away, picked away. And Ulf – picked away and picked away...No! I know! He holds our fate in his hands...Oblivion, Griffin. I'm last! I die, and my blood dies.

As the boat drifts towards the shore, the vision of the climb replays itself to Griffin. It is as if he is trying to remember, by an act of will and stimulated by new evidence, the exact detail of his original vision. The gauntlet begins to emerge as the key. Foregrounded, it convinces Griffin (and, for the moment, us) that it is his brother who will tumble to his death. Panic takes hold of him, and again and again he calls for his brother, while Searle, in his dark rage, tells him, "Without you, we're blind". Nevertheless, the boy jumps overboard.[43] Desperation drives Searle up onto the horse's back, and into the water after him. It is a mark of Ward's grasp as a director that he is prepared to let us feel the mutual fear and confusion of both horse and man in the water as they circle looking for direction in one single sustained shot, just as he is prepared to leave in one unchanging frame, almost immediately afterwards, a wonderfully composed shot, full of pathos, terror and comedy, the night-time city street with traffic circulating in the distance: while Griffin runs towards and through the camera's line of sight, and from the deep distance, with a rattling staccato of hooves, Searle on horseback drives himself with raging momentum into full view in pursuit.

Literally running parallel to the water-crossing, and intercut with it, is Connor's passage by land, which also brings him into contact with *Gargantua*, under the azure monochrome of the basilisk moon. The setting is some kind of universal scrapyard, an "everywhere" of mankind's appetite for the earth's resources, marshalled by the quick descending talons of giant beings. We recognise these lumbering beasts as no more than grab-cranes, or waste trucks or bulldozers, brilliantly choreographed into the frame, but part of the humour and grotesquerie lies in Connor's absurd, terrified response to their movement and noise, mostly desperate flight and an open-mouthed howl. He backs and huddles against a surface, and immediately it springs to life, a diesel locomotive, accelerating away down the tracks with him pinned against its bows in a cruel racket of momentum, his face tortured and twisted by air pressure as thoroughly and as nastily as if by demons. Connor's passage is, in fact, through Pandemonium,[44] and his primal howl is an emblem of the shock inherent to this translation of values, illustrating a mythos within which Man, in the image of God, captures the deity's powers, bends them to his own will in order to free his own will, and creates a third race of beings, the Machines, which, in the exercise of their power, show cognisance of neither God nor Man. As nothing more than a tick, Connor is ejected from the steel skin of the locomotive when it comes to a halt amongst empty station platforms, and is helplessly propelled on his way. Sonorous strokes of a bell have been sounding, and the slim blanched spire of the cathedral has been glimpsed, by both Griffin and Connor, almost insignificant amongst mammoth corporation towers.

Nuclear-free

Dodging behind an early morning rubbish truck and into an arcade, Griffin is abruptly confronted by a mosaic of identical images, streaming off banks of television sets inside a shop. A bird of prey, a hawk, is attacking a hare (another version of merciless talons descending on helpless prey), the constellation of pictures pouring obliquely across the line of sight as the camera pitches and cranes in subtle counterpoint to them, gradually isolating the master-image itself at the point where the hawk flies parallel to Griffin in lubricated slow-motion, its vacant great eye and opened beak of death revealed in sudden documentary immediacy, recalling, and contrasting with, the palpably false plague skeleton that flew over the burrowing men earlier. As Griffin stares, hypnotised, a voice begins to speak, calm and authoritative, and the image of a man appears, hermetically sealed in neutral space, his handkerchief neatly folded into the top jacket pocket of his dark suit, universal corporate man:[45] "The fact is, you still have an alliance with America. This is the real world, 1988, you can't isolate one little particle of the world and say 'nuclear-free'...oh, you can try, but then, there is no refuge, no pocket, no escape from the real world...".[46]

Griffin pushes his gaze towards him, taking the man's image for real, inquiring, "Where is the cathedral?". It is the image which answers him, by dissolving, not into the cathedral tower and spire, but into the conning tower of a nuclear submarine at sea, a behemoth, Hobbes' Leviathan of centralised state power, symbol of humanity's post-technological commonwealth not of salvation, but of beauteous annihilation.[47] In the difference between the medieval plague and contemporary nuclear threat, the first relies upon human ignorance and helplessness, just as the second celebrates the certainties of human knowledge, capability and absolute power; both, however, are fatally blown by the winds of superstition. Ward's black leviathan, foaming to the surface, not only represents what might be an obsessive personal nightmare, but also rises as a growing obsession in the New Zealand national psyche. A small, young country, still seeking identity, can rightly feel helpless (and self-righteous) outrage at how the strategies of death-dealing can covertly shift and slide to the world's farthest corners, so that nothing, nowhere, can avoid becoming simultaneously a launching pad and a target zone – pandemic, in fact. And this is the irony which is at the heart of Ward's film. In finding the means best to escape all manner of biological plagues, humanity nevertheless cannot turn aside a gaze fixated on death-dealing deliverers.

By the time both Searle and Arno have caught up with him, Griffin has thoroughly lost his way. The wealth of immediate impressions, crashing against his outer eye, are drowning the visions of which his inner eye can barely keep sight. "It's like...I see too much". At this point, the published script outlines a clearly ambitious agenda of visual stimuli, of flashing lights and reflected images, the fragmenting electrical detritus of the inner city, with the guiding strokes of the cathedral bell subsiding beneath accumulating din. Onscreen, the effort is much more modest; a passing accident pick-up truck, and, still being mysteriously delayed, a police car. Even more unaccountably, given the almost total absence of people on the streets, is the brief appearance of an unaccompanied blind man, with dark glasses and white cane – the kind of symbolic sign-painting which the film has surely never needed. However, it provides Griffin with the impulse to have his eyes bound; the best way through a maze may not be by sight. This does provide a powerful image, however, of the blind boy, arms outstretched, through city backstreets, precipitously leading the others to their destination.

Aspiring upwards and spiralling downwards

The climactic set-piece of the film takes place at the cathedral, and the first principle of its orchestration is a brilliantly sustained and vertiginous sense of verticality, in which set design, clever stunt work, dynamic framing, inch-perfect editing and exactly orchestrated sound all play their part. The character of the sequence owes much to the very idea of the spire, a piece of architecture whose single purpose is to mark the point in space at which the materiality of life on earth transforms itself into spirit by contact with the heavens, the point into which the spike of the cross is to be placed.[48] In its gradually diminishing materiality, the spire suggests the intoxication of both flight and fall, a position of ultimate vulnerability, a point of no return. Flight is to journey away from the thrall of the past, to enter new realms, to voyage on the arrow of history. To fall is to return, damaged and broken, to mundane circumstance, trapped into the closed circle of necessary ritual. It says a great deal of Ward as a filmmaker that he can so intuitively take his characters, in this film as in others, from a state of earth-boundness and earth-buriedness to a freedom of elevation, by way of difficult corridors and thresholds, and chart in these journeys the complex and ambiguous theme of aspiration, that steadfast desire in the human heart for an attainment, a state of grace and knowledge, beyond all present circumstance. Connor's impetuous momentum has already thrown him, unthinkingly, halfway up the precipitous route to a final passageway. He now hangs in space, one hand on a rope ladder, the other searching for control of the rope which, driven by a motorised winch on the back of Smithy's truck, is hauling aloft the newly-minted copper cross, Martin and the workshop men having arrived at the cathedral without apparent difficulty.

But, as Griffin shouts up, "Don't move!", to his brother the instant the blindfold is removed, and he and Searle charge through the door into the church and up the winding stone spiral staircase – the camera always behind them in the rush, framed on feet – the rope shreds and snaps, the cross breaks loose from its leash, and begins to swing in towards Connor in his difficulty, falling onto him, as if beating him, punishing him, driving him downwards. Connor's will is encountering another kind of presence - call it "God" or fate - which plainly does not want him to triumph, and it tortures him, smashing him brutally down through the rungs of the ladder, one by one. And almost as soon as Searle lays his hand on the rungs, and starts to climb to Connor's aid, the two of them are summarily dealt with; Searle finally hanging upside-down over infinity, a parody of the universal figure of The Hanged Man.[49] Griffin's arrival at the base of the ladder is announced by a beautiful visual caesura, the moon suddenly framed, still, staring, in the parallelogram of the opened doorway to the heavens, while into the suspended moment finally we hear for the first time the banal concerto of arriving police and ambulance sirens. The moment is extended into a held long-shot of the tower and spire, with the ladder and rope marking an absolute vertical down the skin of the building: Searle at the bottom and hanging on, Griffin in the middle, Connor above, the furious curses of the men spitting into the empty wind, with the sinking moon behind them.

This action sequence has been assembled at breakneck pace, with explosive close-up sound detail and driving orchestral music, exploiting conventional suspense elements, and emphasising how Connor's gloved hand once or twice loses its grip as he tumbles - confirming, it seems, Griffin's prophecy. Now, as Griffin begins to climb, a different rhythm establishes itself, his steady upward motion contrasting with the broken resolve of Connor. So much in the brief negotiation between the two brothers is displayed through the play of Connor's eyes, always quick and mobile, even in the personal defeat he has just suffered. A close-up has already re-emphasised Griffin's bandaged hand reaching up the rungs, and the same close-up which earlier established the gauntlet as a key element in the narrative now also frames the transference of it from Connor to Griffin. It is a gesture of simple caring concern on the part of the older brother, but one which binds the two of them unequivocally into the final decisive steps of the adventure; this time, it is Griffin who mouths the motto between them, "Godspeed". Unlike Connor's frenzied energy earlier, Griffin's ascent is measured, sustained, hand over hand (in which detail we must recognise, if we have not already, the fatal significance of the gauntlet), hearing the boy's breath and effort, the intimate sound of the hand grasping each rung, accompanied by a pure, solicitous solo woman's voice on the soundtrack, the spike rising alongside him, hauled aloft by the steady horse which has replaced the unreliable engine. As, in pre-dawn silhouette, the boy labours at the top of his climb, we are suddenly joined again to the lives of the Cumbrian villagers, Linnet and Chrissie making their way urgently forwards through the snow to greet the news of the mission. "Dawn's coming, for good or ill", exclaims Linnet. The shot is startlingly, glowingly, in colour, a return to the merged realities of Griffin's original dream, and suddenly every image is suffused with the yellows and blood-reds of the rising sun, the blue of night vanished, an echoing voice hailing the moment, which, fatally for Griffin, comes just seconds in advance of the spike slipping into its mount with absolute percussion. The shouts of celebration, the tumultuous voice of bells, and the sun racing upwards above the clouds allow for a momentary breath of immortality, in which, as Linnet approaches and gazes through the frame, past and present are locked together: "They're safe".

But only for the instant of Griffin's whoop of joy. The sky's glow is also the brute colour of mortal flesh, perpetually infected by death. Slowly, exquisitely, his grip is lost, and from below we see the brief passage of his downward fall, a bundle of rags, inconsequential against the firm skyward thrust of the tower and the spike. His single extended scream translates between times and realities, black-and-white images reasserting themselves against the memory of colour. The gauntlet, as it flies down through the wind-chilled air like the shadow of a hawk, emptied of all grasp, is suddenly in black-and-white, marker of the irreducible present. There has been a dream, a vision; but, in reality, nothing has yet been accomplished.

Eternal return

After the lush, sensuous, translucent, energetic experience of colour, the return to the group in the damp darkness of the mine, immobile, shocked, with only the play of the flames' light upon their faces, is expertly restrained. The amount of screen time spent on the sequence is just as much to allow us, as them, to come back to themselves. Martin, as always, catches, in a single precise phrase, the fact that the boy has held them, through the night, in the thrall of a story: "It was – like a window opened". Only the resolution to Ulf's role in the venture allows a brief, comic and touching coda, a return to the world of the 20th century, in which, true to his calling as a miner, the big man trenches his way across the motorway, the traffic roaring over him; and, true to the modesty of his soul, he holds his little Virgin to a sight of the incommensurable city. Nevertheless, the expression of a feminine presence is only to be allowed, it seems, a second-tier seat, a distant eye on the deeds of heroes. The dwindling light is a mere pinprick in Griffin's eyes. As for Searle, now he is back on terra firma, he has no doubts about the experience: "A vision of hell...".

Again it is Ulf that we follow into a sequence, his face boiling with pleasure, his stagger and trot taking him up through the village and its accumulating celebration, a right-to-left pan, in which the settlement appears rich in texture and figures, reminding us in panorama of what has been throughout the film the simply detailed and evocative production design of Sally Campbell, the whole thing exploding out along the horizon line like a Pieter Bruegel painting. The music is high-stepping, an invigorating dance. "God's spared us all...The moon's already down and no one's fallen ill – no one", Searle is told. "The dream...?", mutters Searle, and the others, their faces softened and all but smiling, avow the efficacy of their shared adventure, although Connor begins to move away with that same ambiguous backward glance which seems always to suggest retribution in his train. Griffin is in the midst of the skirl, twirling his coat above his head like a bull-roarer (a sound that is deliberately caught, evoking the sound of both the flying skeleton and the cruel hawk). Then we hear his breath begin to catch and labour, and a point-of-view shot suggests a loss of balance. In close-up, his hand reaches down to his opposite arm, and a sharp gasp of pain marks contact with the bubo. The script has him whispering "Plague...", but in the film it is "Death..." which he mouths. His panicking mind picks out the moment of reunion when he asked his brother "You won't go away like that no more, Connor, will you?", and Connor lies, "No, never"; and then not just a single blow, but two, which Connor delivers, now much more afraid and defensive than we noticed the first time, as he suddenly gets up and leaves the group after the black motorway, in the dream; and then the image of the cast spike floating in or under shimmering water, now ambiguous and insubstantial, like the bacillus of plague itself. Against the bleak monochrome of the boy's white face, these images are in colour, confusing utterly any simple notion of what is "reality" and what "dream". Cleverly, Ward plays the moment of realisation not on Griffin's face, but on the reaction to him on the face of the little girl who is his admirer. "Death", he repeats; then "Connor".

Cunningly, Ward evokes the pain of Griffin's deepening realisation of his brother's betrayal by extending the distance between the two of them across the excruciating exposure of these northern hills – firstly by a long zoom over snow towards the icy lake, in shivering pursuit of Connor and Linnet, whose path has taken them away in the closest to dalliance that life here has to offer; and then in two or three following shots of the laborious passage through the deep snow that Griffin has to take to reach them. On the other hand, the moment of Connor's unmasking is instant and abrupt; the mark on his neck tells all. Everything is suddenly compressed, conveyed through the barest of notation - Griffin's ferocity; the sound of Linnet's lamentation; the retreat of Griffin's smaller brothers; the quick appearance of Arno, Searle and Ulf. Connor's words in defence, on a personal level, suggest the dimension of tragedy; a moral predicament to which there is to be no outcome but disaster, and Bruce Lyons here gives his character its culminating touches - dignified, fearful, vulnerable. But his speech also highlights a collective predicament which has always been itching at human consciousness - the trapped circularity of the extended post-tribal community, an absolute dependency and need which, at the same time, knows all too well the pull of destiny, and pushes itself, in a kind of mortal terror, into the directionality we call history, daring itself to encounter change, and to experience the movement "away" from centre which we have come, for good or for ill, to call progress:

> Griffin, I swear I didn't know plague was upon me...Not till we were in the pit, and then I kept my distance...from all of you, I swear it, and I was afraid...There was nothing else I could do...you understand? There was nowhere else for me to go...and I came to believe the unfolding of your story was...I came to believe it was my salvation...the salvation of us all...

These final moments in the drama of *The Navigator* suggest a paradigm for the collective assimilation of notions of a secular salvation, and it is the fierce voice of the doomed Griffin, wise beyond his years, who insists on it.[50] His own life is forfeit, nipped in the bud, sacrificed; but, through the agency of his damned brother, the community will come to know in detail the events of the story, and they will be remembered. And perhaps acted upon. And perhaps, in such a way, the future, one way or another, will be reached. The important point is that there is one. Death is not absolute. A navigation around Death is possible, impelled through the unconscious in the shape of visions, and brought to consciousness within the community in the shape of stories, maps and journeys made complete.

The final moments of the film, heralded by a quick fade

through black, reprise elements of the very first sequence. Griffin's face in close-up, his eyes drifting in and out of focus. One or two shots in colour, proposing that this is still his "dream", but mingling indiscriminately with the black-and-white reality to suggest, at the moment of his own death, that the two are now one, indistinguishable. As the coffin is pushed out onto the water, towards the world of Death, and Searle mutters, "Travel well, boy", the image of the cross glimmers under the water, tantalisingly close, as a symbol of promise, in the world of Life. The camera pans one last time over the faces of Griffin's companions, upon whom the future now weighs. Linnet's newborn child utters its helpless cry. Connor's "Godspeed" is uttered as a benediction to his lost brother over water, but, as the story fades from view, we get the feeling that the solemnity of the moment, ennobled by the dark emotive pulse of Davood A Tabrizi's score, is an equally devout wish for the happiness and prosperity of those who remain on shore. As Ward has said:

> I believe faith and hope are pre-requisites for action and change, regardless of the odds. Not in the sense of religious hope and faith, but in the sense of faith in the potential of human creativity.[51]

Critical reception

Milan Kundera has observed in defence of the art of literary criticism, "without it a work is surrendered to completely arbitrary judgments and swift oblivion".[52] Media comment has an undoubted effect on the immediate commercial viability of a feature film, as does festival success, without either necessarily defining or penetrating a film's sustaining qualities. *The Navigator*'s first public audience was at the Cannes Film Festival in 1988, New Zealand's first-ever official entry in competition, where, according to *The Weekend Australian*'s Phillip Adams, "[t]here was a crescendo of acclamation. A standing ovation that went on and on and on, one of the warmest responses I've heard in a lifetime at the Festival".[53]

This enthusiasm was picked up by Jean Faydit de Terssac in his piece for *Aspects de la France* directly on the heels of Cannes, expressing complete contempt, in a year that was "dull on the whole", towards the festival jury for failing to award the Palme D'Or to the film: "We are dealing here with an exemplary specimen of pure cinema. Vincent Ward possesses to the greatest degree the quality which should be the basic quality of every film-maker worthy of the name: the sense of the visual."[54]

This concentration on the visual was very much taken up by critics generally: "real visual flair"; "rich with primitive images"; "a rare mastery of the diversity and beauty of the images"; "astonishing aesthetic depth"; "in terms of originality and vision a rare piece of cinema"; "visionary force". But press response also admired the film's thematic ambition and risk. Keith Connolly, in a feature in *The Sydney Herald*, wrote: "To call it 'original' is, in film-making terms, something of an understatement";[55] the same city's *Daily Mirror* battled with the very idea of such chutzpah from a work of entertainment: "It is difficult to put this film into a category. It has the power to set anyone thinking and feeling and wondering"[56] - about what precisely it does not have to elucidate. *Variety* was impressed by the best sequences affirming "the timeless ascendancy of individual human spirit against the forces that would dehumanize",[57] and many of the notices were characterised by a sort of amazement that such a film should emanate from one of the film world's remoter poles. Sean French in *The Observer* emerged from the Edinburgh Festival screening of the film a wiser man: "I must confess that before last week I was only dimly aware of the New Zealand film industry".[58] Philip French in the same newspaper was convinced that Ward "is an antipodean Werner Herzog";[59] and the writer in the *Sydney Sun Herald* expressed sheer astonishment that something locally produced could be a "complex dazzling film, ambitiously conceived and confidently executed", and plainly not just "doomed to poky late-night screenings in Artsville, France", usefully hitting the perennial paradox of how self-conscious art can enter the commercial mainstream, the problem for Herzog, Tarkovskij *et al.*[60] No such wool-pulling for another Sydney reviewer, Peter Crayford, in *The Sydney Review*, who, in one of the few unfavourable pieces, likened it to Beineix's cult movie, *Diva* (1980), as "much ado about not very much. Style dominates content, contrivance replaces character, and the result is visually arresting but vapid."[61] While admiration for the film's crafting - the contribution of Simpson's cinematography, Campbell's production design and Tabrizi's score - was generally unanimous, there was the occasional quibble about its clarity and consistency of theme; Derek Malcolm in *The Guardian* found it had "daft and pretentious moments", and that the film "often trips up over itself",[62] while one or two were even willing to trace out the likely reasons for such weaknesses. The writer in the *Australian FilmNews* suggested that "some of the analogies are too neat and not well thought through, and I think that the second part could have been slightly longer to retain the emotive links with the characters",[63] while the same country's *Sunday Press* critic was of the opinion that "strangely, the 14th century scenes are more convincing than those set in the present day", felt let down by "the bland 20th century" sequences, and found that it was not "easy to get what Vincent Ward is aiming at, and sometimes his aim appears a little astray",[64] again without spelling out any detail on the mis-aim. In one of the few sustained pieces of critical writing on Ward's work to appear subsequently, Michael Wilmington in *Film Comment*'s somewhat slapdash style, nevertheless makes good and wary judgment when it counts:

> Like the post-*Strangelove* Stanley Kubrick, Ward works so infrequently, with such monomaniacal determination, perfectionism, and ambition, that too much mystique may burden each new release. And the objet d'art stylistics of his films – the compositions suitable for framing, the rapt slow rhythms, the gorgeously cool color, and enigmatic, symbolic characters and situations – may burden them as well: especially for critics incensed at other critics they think are suckers for objets d'art, or for uplifting hymns to the human spirit, to which Ward also may be prone.[65]

But not forgetting the dream

Ward has said that his film provides "a collision, a sort of juxtaposition of two time periods which enables you to see your own time through fresh eyes".[66] The thread of this study has been to suggest that *The Navigator*, through its narrative energy and visual acuity, by folding themes of terror, faith, will and technology through each other – the plague as catalyst, the engine as means, the cross as lure, and so on – describes the technical evolution of modern times as a complex moral fable, in which the best impulses, intentions and actions create a pathway to cheat Death's overwhelming presence. At the same time, it suggests ingenuity as an ambivalent human power, and deviousness as an inevitable companion of it. While the risk-laden journey is undertaken in innocent appeal to God's mercy and grace, it is the "Devil's bargain" which accrues. "Innocent" Griffin is sacrificed; "cunning" Connor survives. However, as the French writer Hélène Cixous observes:

> Like plants, dreams have enemies, plant lice that devour them. The dream's enemy is interpretation.[67]

It is a mark of Ward's courage to engage with ambitious themes within the extremely limited canvas of the commercial feature film, to do so uncompromisingly, and a particular miracle that he is able to find finance and support. But the film is also superbly crafted, given over to the sheer lyricism of sound and image in conjunction; impelled by its narrative thrust, but also graphic, sensuous, emotive, haunting, so that we are compelled to lose ourselves in it, excitedly, uncomprehendingly. As Cixous says:

> We must know how to treat the dream as a dream, to leave it free, and to distrust all the exterior and interior demons that destroy dreams...We must let ourselves be carried on the dream's mane and must not wake up - something all dreamers know - while the dream is dictating the world to us...You have to take a rock, put it under your head, and let the dream ladder grow. It grows down - toward the depths.[68]

And upwards towards the heights.

Notes

1 It would be true to say that in contemporary New Zealand a certain postcolonial sense of guilt inhabits the Pākehā sensibility, particularly in relation to a continuing upsurge of Māori identity and culture. This can produce a severe undervaluation of a dense European heritage, except in the multifaceted operation of the "cultural cringe" towards Europe still operating onshore within the country's institutions, and as a celebration carried on offshore through the traditional "overseas experience" of many young New Zealanders of British or European descent. Ward has made it clear that *The Navigator* makes no apology for its claim on a natural heritage: "we have as much claim to the medieval as the English do, or the French, or anybody else. In terms of the majority of pakehas living in this country our relationship is as direct as is an Englishman's. We may not have the same buildings here, but we are directly descended...Some people assume that pakeha culture is not a rich thing. This simply isn't true. Although colonial cultures have similarities, each one brought different things with them. They're fed from different roots which they combine with the fresh

influences of their new country and its people." Quoted in "A Dialogue with Discrepancy: Vincent Ward Discusses *The Navigator*", interview by Russell Campbell and Miro Bilbrough, *Illusions* 10 (March 1989): 11.

2 This presented itself "as a play of tensions, silences and repressions, in which the author is a problematic 'inscription' rather than an intentional source of meaning, a personality or a principle of unity". John Caughie (ed), *Theories of Authorship: A Reader* (London; Boston; Henley: Routledge & Kegan Paul, 1981): 14.

3 Andrej Tarkovskij, the Russian director whose working practice and thematic concerns have much in common with those of Ward, had no fears in expressing this critically unfashionable idea: "He starts to be an artist at the moment when, in his mind or even on film, his own distinctive system of images starts to take shape – his own pattern of thoughts about the external world – and the audience are invited to judge it, to share with the director in his most precious and secret dreams. Only when his personal view-point is brought in, when he becomes a kind of philosopher, does he emerge as an artist, and cinema – as an art." Andrey Tarkovsky, *Sculpting in Time: Reflections on the Cinema*, translated by Kitty Hunter-Blair (London: The Bodley Head, 1986): 60.

4 Ward has said: "It's naive, involves a suspension of disbelief, is very childlike. I wanted a sense of wonder". Michele Nayman, "*The Navigator* – Vincent Ward's past dreams of the future", *Cinema Papers* 69 (May 1988): 31. It should also be pointed out at this stage, at the moment of plunging into a serious-minded exploration of the film's themes, that *The Navigator* is also an essentially playful work of the imagination, with its absurd narrative premise a direct provocation to interpretation, a series of potent images and tableaux which operate as much as fetishistic repetitions and fascinations, in the subversive manner of Surrealism. As Russell Campbell has pointed out in an excellent short article, "[t]he very concept of medieval miners stumbling round Auckland has the lunatic *impossibility* of a flaccid pocketwatch, and the link with the purest of surrealist impulses is there in other ways: in the ludic qualities of the film...in the incongruity of the imagery...in the centrality of Griffin's dream...in the refusal...of the narrative to submit to rational explication". See Russell Campbell, "The Blindfold Seer: Vincent Ward's *Navigator*", *Illusions* 10 (March 1989): 15. Emphasis in original. What militates against a total reading of the film in these terms, as a purely oneiric text, is the directional thrust of the narrative and the deeply embedded moral implications of themes deliberately being worked through.

5 "It's a real jigsaw of a film...every other shot is filmed on a different location, although you'd never think it". Ward, in an interview with Kerry Jimson, *Agenda* 50 (February 1989): 9.

6 "I was hitchhiking through Germany after the 1984 Cannes Film Festival and tried to cross an autobahn where the traffic was going by like artillery fire. I got across three lanes and had four to go when I got stuck, unable to go forwards or backwards. I could see myself in this ridiculous situation, and what it might be like to encounter technology for the first time, like Ulf in the modern world. I finally got back to the side of the road, and thought of a scene for a film. Many New Zealanders going overseas for the first time are trusting and almost medieval in their outlook". Ward, quoted in Terry Snow, "Visionary Force", *The New Zealand Listener* 28 January 1989: 30.

7 The film was eventually shot over a ten-week period, from July to September 1987. Eight of the weeks were night shoots. Ward maintained that it eventually had the highest budget of a "New Zealand" film up to that date, the figure quoted being A$4 300 000.

8 "The boy had to be someone you would believe, someone I could get a day's work out of as an actor, sometimes working waist-deep in water, who looked lean and hardy, cheeky yet a dreamer with a vision...The quality I wanted was hard to find, and it was pure accident that the central role was, as in Vigil, for a child. I originally wrote the part for a 30-year old." Ward, quoted in *The New Zealand Listener* 28 January 1989: 31.

9 His leading actor, Bruce Lyons, himself mostly at the end of his tether, began to parody both Ward and the subject of the film, as alchemist and alchemist's work, respectively: "All the alchemists courted madness or death. They risked injury and poisoning, shut out of the light, subjected to huge temperature variations and horrible stinks. They were dark and eccentric and unless they gave up their egos, they were condemned." See Vincent Ward, with Alison Carter, Geoff Chapple and Louis Nowra, *Edge of the Earth: Stories and Images from the Antipodes* (Auckland: Heinemann Reed, 1990): 172.

10 Griffin's role as the child-seer is obvious within the film, but the dream and mythic dimensions of *The Navigator* provide many possibilities for further speculative interpretation. Judith Dale, in what she describes as "conceptual echoes of Christian, psychological and archaic matri-focal imagery and allegory", has outlined a number of readings on the character and function of Griffin within the story, as a "leader...less of a man than the others; the imagery of J.C. has

always had an other-than-macho, less-than-fully-patriarchal aspect, e.g., as the 'lamb of God'. It is Griffin who a-spires, who climbs the spire to raise the cross, takes up his cross to raise up the cross, as a crowd gathers at its foot." Griffin's "unknowing" self-sacrifice shadows the Christian story, and Dale's comments raise the appropriate questions about how Ward (like Tarkovskij or Paradžanov) might be viewed as a religious artist. From another angle, Dale also validly sees Griffin as "the typified self, an 'Everyman' making what existentialists call 'the leap of faith'". See Judith Dale, "Circumnavigations", *Illusions* 11 (July 1989): 44-45. This commingling of themes helps demonstrate the resonances present in Ward's narrative.

11 John Berger and Jean Mohr, *Another Way of Telling* (London: Writers and Readers, 1982): 118. Emphasis in original.

12 Ibid: 116. Emphasis in original.

13 A final example, in which the essential qualities of appearance, revelation and the legendary are presented with paradigmatic force, is Ward's 1980 version of Janet Frame's story, *State of Seige.* The bourgeois logical-positivist art teacher, much given to depicting the world on neat canvases of identical size, inexplicably shifts herself from familiar surroundings to a remote house by a fierce, isolated shore in order "to see things more clearly". Ward charts her disintegration with stunning simplicity, in a slow, obsessional gaze onto surfaces. As she compels herself against all sense not to look away, the terror of true revelation pitilessly smashes through the fragile membrane of her eyes, splintering her soul as irreparably as a single stone thrown through glass.

14 "[W]hat interested me was to take an area which is not normally explored, which there isn't too much information on, which you have to make a number of deductions on. We tried to find as much information as possible, and then treat it creatively. In actual fact the houses in the village would be much more likely to be stone-built, for warmth. You wouldn't have a wooden house like I've got, where you can see light through the slats, it would be stupid. But I went into this quite consciously." Ward, in "A Dialogue with Discrepancy": 11.

15 "[T]he idea of the antipodes, literally the opposite foot. The belief, which I think was Greek and inherited by the medievals, was that there was a continent at the bottom of the world which matched the continent at the top of the world, an exact mirror image...And there are various stories about what sort of creatures belong in that sphere, that realm. Essentially it comes to the idea of opposites. So

it's a place where the map lines ran out, where land became open lines, the boundaries not defined...A land at the opposite end of the world, only of course it is a land we're familiar with. The audience ironically has a knowledge they [the miners] don't have." Ward, in ibid: 10.

16 Dale (44), in her interpretations which show a shadowing of the story of Christ within *The Navigator*, suggests that Connor "plays a kind of Simon of Cyrene when he carries the cross part of the way; earlier he is a John-the-Baptist, forerunner-and-proclaimer; finally he is a death figure and maybe even the necessary Judas".

17 Barbara W Tuchman, *A Distant Mirror: The Calamitous 14th Century* (London; Basingstoke: Macmillan, 1979): 123.

18 Ibid: 124. *The Navigator* evokes the raw life, sensibilities and visions of medieval times, and sets itself completely within the classic tradition of Judaeo-Christian apocalypse; a work in dream form, which reveals or approaches some superior authority, is eschatologically orientated, and constitutes a criticism of, and warning for, contemporary society. The most famous, and most idiosyncratic, model in the Anglo-Saxon tradition is Thomas Langland's *Piers Plowman*, which lays out a narrative vision in which Will and Conscience are in search of a spiritual knowledge that will transform both society and the self. The poem deals with the search and not the finding; and, although the quest, of both Will and Conscience, will not be in vain, the goal has yet to be attained. At the same time, it is made plain within this visionary poem that salvation is to be found at both personal and social levels; in other words, in terms of a general social regeneration, indicating the root of utopian energies which run through English social thinking to the 20th century, and which are present to Ward through the social engineering experiments which helped create modern New Zealand. *The Navigator* makes particular play for a material knowledge which will transform society, and leaves the spiritual dimension (with its medieval notions of Virtue and Sin) morally ambiguous – more *Piers Engineer* than *Piers Plowman*, perhaps.

19 "There are times...when you want to wring his neck. But then you see the results, and the results are very distinctive". Geoffrey Simpson, in Nayman: 30.

20 The images in the film at this point, however, seem briefer, more confused and less stark than the suggestions made in the published edition of the script: "On board the burning boat a WOMAN tears the flaming tunic from her chest. As she flings herself towards the water we see that her body is partially covered in enormous black

buboes. Now we see that the faces around her are similarly covered in obscene welts. The refugees...are pushed, by the distant villagers, at spear's point deeper into the water. Laden down with clothing, unable to swim, frozen with cold, in some cases clinging to floating animals and other flotsam, they struggle in vain to save themselves from drowning." Vincent Ward, Kely Lyons and Geoff Chapple, *The Navigator: A Medieval Odyssey* (London; Boston: Faber and Faber, 1989): 16.

21 Ward is also sensitive to the political dimensions inherent in his characters as agents of social change: "medieval miners had a position that other feudal peasants did not have, and by and large they were called free miners. They had effectively 'union' rights, they had mining rights on virtually any land, and they were better paid, and the reason was war was at such a peak. For armaments metal was essential, and for metal you needed miners. So they had a very privileged position in society. The fourteenth century saw the beginning of the emancipation of working people in general. This was caused by the Black Death, because it brought about labour shortages, which in turn meant that people had more bargaining power. So in the film there is a link between common working people then and now, the medieval miners being at the forefront of the change in working-class conditions." Ward, in "A Dialogue with Discrepancy": 10-11. This is obviously an important point to consider when the miners encounter the modern-day foundry workers later in the film, but it also reminds us that human inventiveness and social change are mostly driven, then as now, by war industries.

22 In general, both filmmakers and audiences perceive black-and-white photography as signifying a particular stage within the evolution of film technology (approximately from the 1890s to the 1950s), which in turn spawned particular kinds of genre and expressivity within the overall history of the medium, as a kind of "classical" period. Colour photography, on the other hand, is one of the signs which represent the cinema's coming of age as a medium of true spectacle and impact, the high precision and definition of which guarantee a film as a viable commercial product in the modern world. While colour images within film fictions can both glamourise and romanticise the surface of things, the black-and-white image has almost always retained its integrity as providing notions of a certain truth-to-life within a documentary depiction of events, whether factual or fictional. Filmmakers within the highly quotational cinema (and television) of the postmodern period evolving since the early 1970s will always feel free to plunder the image bank of cinema history – an employment of visual play which can often be spurious or meretricious, or both – but interplay between monochrome and

colour images will usually be used to highlight either historicity (i.e. of a time existing before the strictly modern) or factuality (i.e. of events which possess a truth, an integrity, beyond the melodramatic allure of panchromaticism).

23 In his 1986 film, Wenders employs a high-contrast black-and-white cinematography to depict the phenomenalistic environment of guardian angels, constructing an extremely detailed documentation of the everyday surfaces of Berlin, both past and present, which is simultaneously the territory of "supernatural" beings who conventionally would be excluded from such a documentary notion of the world. On the other hand, colour in this film is used to evoke an eternal, yet mortal and sensual, present: the one we experience entirely from within our own skin, within our own lifetime; the one in which we can do something as simple as rub our own hands together for warmth, or as complex as having a sense of entering one's own irrevocable destiny. In other words, the interplay between colour and monochrome is not only a decoration or a technical effect, but also intrinsic to Wenders' purpose within the film medium, indicating the strong philosophical directions of his themes. Tarkovskij's astounding epic, based on the 12th-century Russian icon painter, depicts a number of fictional episodes from Andrej's life – sudden, brief, brutal, austere – shot in pellucid black-and-white, which, for all its stylistic adventurings, nevertheless conveys as documentary and as earthbound a sense of a remote historical time as exists in all cinema. A key moment occurs at the end of the final episode (which itself is based around the visionary intuitions of a boy). Andrej is sitting by the dying embers of an outdoor fire. A dissolve moves us through this image to the first in a series of visual excursions across the surfaces of the historical Andrej's paintings, the real paintings, and they explode out at us in their living colour. The dialectic created here allows us to consider the spiritual dimensions of art (very much a central concern through all of Tarkovskij's films): how such images of inward contemplation and certainty could have been created by a man living his life amidst such base cruelty and desperate insecurity, and, on a broader level, how temporality and permanence are woven together inextricably.

24 The palaeontologist Stephen Jay Gould has summarised a contemporary state of knowledge defining principles of biological evolution as possessing "punctuated equilibrium": "Obviously, for a revised view about the general tempo of evolutionary change, stasis can provide only one side of a story, lest we be left with no evolution at all! The opposite and integrated side (the punctuation in punctuated equilibrium) proposes a concentration of change into relatively short episodes – jabs of reorganization in a world of generally stable systems. Enter this world at any random moment

and, as an overwhelming probability, nothing much will be happening in a history of change. But survey the totality over millions of years, and these episodes of punctuation, though they may occupy only a percent or two of time, build the signature of historical alteration. Scale is everything in history and geology." Stephen Jay Gould, *Dinosaur in a Haystack: Reflections in Natural History* (London: Jonathan Cape, 1996): 142. What is true of this genetic realm might be usefully transposed to the exogenetic or cultural realm, through which the evolution of human history is to be traced, although cultural change is highly accelerated compared to the biological, a matter of centuries, generations and, these days, perhaps even hours.

25 Searle mutters: "I think you've got us all sleepwalking, old son...", recalling the title, *The Sleepwalkers*, which Arthur Koestler gave to his account of Copernicus, Kepler and Galileo making their revolutionary impact upon Western cosmology, one of the bases of the Western scientific world-view, at a time not so very many years distant from the date suggested by Ward for *The Navigator*.

26 Ward says that the engine was based on medieval technology, citing Jean Gimpel's book, *The Medieval Machine: The Industrial Revolution of the Middles Ages* (London: Victor Gollancz, 1977) as a source, and that it closely resembles the trebuchet, a medieval catapult.

27 The word "sublime" has many connotations, one of which might refer here to the perfect appositeness of two pieces of celluloid joined together, a jump cut, arrived at by both narrative expediency and thematic necessity. But it is worth considering how this sequence of tunnelling provides access to a broader sense of the sublime. *The Navigator* possesses many aspects of an adventure story, pure and simple, but it has an ambition of theme, typical of Ward's films as a whole, which relates strongly to ideas of the Romantic Sublime, to an aspiring sense of humanity, in which the human adventure in the world is to be characterised by feelings of exultation, awe and scale – a heightening, a taking to lofty levels – in which intellectuality and spirituality are combined to locate, in the early 19th-century words of William Wordsworth (a Cumbrian, like Ward's miners) in "The Prelude", as "something evermore about to be". (Quoted in "Neoclassic and Romantic", in M H Abrams, *A Glossary of Literary Terms*, sixth edition [Fort Worth: Harcourt Brace College Publishers, 1993]: 129.) Implied within this view is a positivist projection of human progress, standing at the beginning of the 19th century, in which both political and technological revolutions were straining at their various leashes, the linchpin century which greatly accelerated the transformation of marginal societies into the mass societies, even the global society, of the present day. Etymologically, the word

"sublime" collides two possible roots: limus (oblique) and limen (threshold), thus triggering a sense of "crossing over", or through, or more literally (sub-) "under"; hence, perhaps, "coming under the threshold from an unlikely direction" might be a way of describing the "punctuations" of technological progress within history, as well as the basic premise of Ward's film, with this sequence, and this cut which heralds it, at its heart. Perhaps the most sublime cut in movie history, in this sense, is the one made by Stanley Kubrick in *2001: A Space Odyssey* (1968), in which an animal bone thrown into the air by an intelligent ape transforms instantly into a space station circling the earth, and the total moment of human evolution is elegantly and dynamically apparent, one linking temporal poles even more remote in time and place from each other than those being fused together in *The Navigator*. The passage of place and time, the threshold, in Ward's film is plainly more laboriously achieved; Ward has more time for the mere sweat of humanity than the cool, more cerebral and more fatalistic Kubrick. Of course, there is yet another value to "sublimation" – that provided by empirical science in which a substance is translated from its very baseness, through heat, into something gaseous, vaporous and free-flowing, and then, having passed through this purification, is resolidified, redeposited, in another form or place (both actually, as a chemical process, and metaphorically, as an alchemical principle). This again relates obviously to the working endeavours of the primitive industrialists who are the central characters of the film (portable flame is a ubiquitous visual accompaniment to nearly all their actions), but is also another kind of way of viewing, as metaphor, the colour sequences within it; as something momentarily immaterial, in transit from one state to another, neither precisely this nor that, neither a personal hallucination nor a collective reality. The flight of the narrative towards these aspects of sublimity is doing so in order to overcome the preposterous premise that two locations, in time and place, can be linked, literally, by the action of digging down into the earth. The point being driven at here is that it is not just a matter of the imaginative crafting which would accompany any fictional work, but that, in his *mise en scène*, Ward is stirring at the thematic centre of his film, a concept of history which pits passive fatalism with active intervention, as matters of both faith and technology.

28 "The scene was filmed in a three-storey set in an Auckland studio, then a model was made and painted identically so a computer-programmed camera enabled the studio scenes to be inset in the cliff face. Back-projection, handmade moon and clouds being moved separately, 30 different machine sounds, impact sounds and blasts of dust synchronised with the 'hits' added to the weeks of shooting and many people involved." The entire composite shot was inspired by the style of engravings in the medieval *De Re Metallica* (1556) by

Georgius Agricola. See Snow: 30. "It was the shot that got me involved in the first place, and we worked like hell to get it right... Vincent was totally void of visual effects knowledge...But that can be a plus for a director. They don't recognise any limitations – they just go for what they want. For me, it was great. It meant having to come up with new ways to achieve the effects Vincent wanted." Visual effects director Paul Nichola, "In Search of the Effect", *Onfilm* 5: 3 (April/May 1988): 9-10.

29 To the medieval mind, this is overwhelmingly true, of course, in ways which our contemporary habituations make hard for us to comprehend, although the irony of this relating to the lateral urban sprawl of a modern city (such as Auckland, the city featured), its open boundaries constantly being shifted by the automobile, might be lost on Martin. Even if he had ever been to a city in his own time, the constrained verticality of the medieval walled city would not have prepared him for this very horizontal kind of vastness.

30 It is natural that the terms of the story should have the tunnellers break through into sewers (another city – antipodean Melbourne, for example – might have had them falling into the subway system), for the sewer represents one of the largest engineering propositions for virtually every city plan since the Romans, however clumsily and imperfectly realised. Allied later to the engineered provision of piped pollution-free water to the industrialising towns and cities of the early 19th century, the removal of massive amounts of human detritus suggests a very particular kind of "mapping" between "plague" and health, the route between helpless decimation and active self-help – given that many epidemic diseases are water-borne – a very necessary direction to be journeyed by technologically evolving mankind.

31 Presumably one of the kinds of detail for which Ward is notorious, creeping into the production, and staying there.

32 In *De Civitate Dei*, St Augustine, within a sort of primer of Christianity, four-square on its pillars of Pax, Ordo, Lex and Societas, repositivised the ideal city which Plato saw as only an ideal, which man's presence endlessly corrupted and made irrevocably remote. The Augustine city is an interpenetration of the civitas Dei with the terrena civitas, the divine commonwealth of heaven with the human commonwealths on earth, finally to produce "such felicity of living and reigning as there shall also be serenity and facility of obeying; and this shall there, in all and in each, be eternal, and its eternity shall be sure; and therefore the peace of this beatitude, or the beatitude of this peace, shall be the Supreme Good". There is a moment's apprehension of this state later in *The*

Navigator, nothing longer than the intake of a breath, when, as sunrise dispels night, the cross has been placed in its socket by Griffin, and the mission is completed.

33 The history of "maps" illustrates a complex weave of relationships between "here", "across", "beneath", "beyond", and so forth. Navigators were, in time, to translate such subjectivity of observation towards the more precise objectivity of latitude and longitude – James Cook, the prime European traverser of antipodean regions, with John Harrison's chronometers aboard, not the least amongst them.

34 For many contemporary social philosophers, an ability continually to accelerate defines both the industrialised modern and the reindustrialised postmodern. Paul Virilio argues that Western "democracies" are more accurately described as "dromocracies" – dromo meaning "running" or "racing" – in which the relationship of speed to power precedes that of wealth to power: "The one who goes the fastest possesses the ability to collect taxes, the ability to conquer, and through that to inherit the right of exploiting society." Paul Virilio and Sylvère Lotringer, *Pure Wars*, revised edition, translated by Mark Polizzotti (New York: Semiotext[e], 1983): 44. Dromocratic society is thus characterised by the reduction of space to time: "The violence of speed has become both the location and the law, the world's destiny and its destination". Paul Virilio, *Speed and Politics: An Essay on Dromology*, translated by Mark Polizzotti (New York: Semiotext[e], 1986): 151. Gilles Deleuze and Félix Guattari extend the idea both abstractly and geometrically: "Laminar movement that striates space, that goes from one point to another, is weighty; but rapidity, celerity, applies only to movement that deviates to the minimum extent and thereafter assumes a vortical motion, occupying a smooth space, actually drawing smooth space itself". Gilles Deleuze and Félix Guattari, *A Thousand Plateaus: Capitalism and Schizophrenia*, translated by Brian Massumi (London: The Athlone Press, 1988): 371. Perhaps one of the weaknesses in the second part of Ward's film is the fact that he only very inconsistently evokes the nature of these vortices of speed.

35 In a speech from the sequence in the published script, but not included in the film, Searle, for whom kinship is a central concern, saw this as a prime fault in Connor: "You who don't give a bloody damn about anything except your God-forsaken wanderings all over Hell's half-kingdom – that's the top of *your* list, isn't it?! Then your family and everything else underneath *that*...". Ward, Lyons and Chapple: 30. Emphases in original.

36 Lewis Mumford has been the most comprehensive and optimistic

chronicler of the rise of the city, and its eloquent defender as a seat of evolving civilisation: "Through its concentration of physical and cultural power, the city heightened the tempo of human intercourse and translated its products into forms that could be stored and reproduced. Through its monuments, written records, and orderly habits of association, the city enlarged the scope of all human activities, extending them backwards and forwards in time. By means of its storage facilities...the city became capable of transmitting a complex culture from generation to generation...the unification of man's inner and outer life...Without the city modern man would have no effective defenses against those mechanical collectives that, even now, are ready to make all veritably human life superfluous, except to perform a few subservient functions that the machine has not yet mastered." Lewis Mumford, *The City in History: Its Origins, Its Transformations, and Its Prospects* (London: Secker & Warburg, 1961): 569-570. However, he was writing before the atomisation of much of the city's function, the result of exploding populations, the rise of contemporary corporates, electronic communication systems, and so on.

37 The published script immediately at this point has Tom assuming "Māoris?", the kind of bare remark that would not endear itself too much to the contemporary sensitivity of Aotearoans, broadly alert to issues of biculturalism, but certainly more acerbic than its unlikely replacement in the film itself, "What's this then? Hare bloody Krishna?". In fact, these three workers are to be the sole representatives of the contemporary city, and, while the choice of them allows the film to establish certain sympathies between past and present, a disconnection between the people of now and then might have produced opportunities for a less attuned, and more satiric and disruptive turn of events.

38 "What would happen if one long dark night your Celtic ancestors came out here, and what if even more distant ancestors of them came along and took a sidelong glance at you? What would they make of where you live? Where would they think they have arrived?". Ward, interview with Jimson.

39 An important piece of dialogue not included in the film conveys this directly, when Smithy says: "I think it's something we'd almost forgotten...love of the trade. It'd make you cry. The night they close us down is the night – I dunno – something comes along to show you how wonderful it could have been." Ward, Lyons and Chapple: 38.

40 The particular and intense luminosity which characterises the colour sequences as a whole, and which reaches its epiphany in the smoky

blues and gilded brilliance of this sequence, represents, of course, a cinematographic strategy which Ward has described clearly: "the twentieth century had to be portrayed in medieval colours. The blues used by the Limbourg brothers in the Duc de Berry's *Book of Hours* I used in the azure of roadside telephone boxes, police car lights and the moonlight grey-blue apparition of a nuclear submarine...This blue is contrasted with the fiery, hellish tones of Bosch, Brueghel and Grünewald. The fires of medieval torches – the sodium from the orange lights of the motorway and the burning gold of molten metal." Ward, Lyons and Chapple: xiii. But Ward is also at pains to point out, given the shooting schedule, how difficult realising this visual aspect proved to be: "No, I never achieved what I wanted to in the twentieth century in terms of colour...To achieve everything I wanted to it would have taken another five weeks, given that I wanted an extra scene and things like that. Three extra scenes I cut, simply because of time. No, I never achieved fully what I wanted to...I got about fifty per cent, perhaps...Whereas in the medieval scenes, I think we got there, in terms of the style." Ward, in "A Dialogue with Discrepancy": 13.

41 One can imagine, for example, an encounter with a sceptical police force, or a street gang in search of drugs or contest, or representatives of the invisible army of night workers who service the corporate gloss of the daytime city, or sustained exposure to the seamless flow of products and images within the culture of excess: something to trigger difficulty, complexity or dialectic within this main body of the narrative.

42 There is an essential quality to the white horse, but it remains too universal to provide a specific interpretation. Pagan horse worship was common, and held a strong power within Celtic tradition – for example, the kings of Ireland were ferried between this world and the next within the womb of the White Mare, Epona, and it is this white horse which is drawn in the chalk at Uffington in Berkshire, England. Ward's obvious fascination with the animal recalls Tarkovskij's similar employment of its presence in several of his films, both as an expression of a (literally) unbridled source of libidinous energy, and as a harbinger of separation or death.

43 The published script contains a hint of a slightly different orientation to this sequence than is realised in the film, reinforcing the surreal aspects to suggest a total emphasis on the events as Griffin's dream. Thus, when Griffin jumps underwater, "he sinks like a stone", and, more interestingly, "Underwater, GRIFFIN begins to walk towards shore on the bottom. He can see the horse's belly on the surface above him." Ward, Lyons and Chapple: 54.

44 The distinctive iconography of this sequence recalls the sort of philosophical enquiry that another filmmaker, the Englishman Humphrey Jennings, quite close in both artistic temperament and subject-matter to Ward, carried on throughout his working life into the matter and spirit of (English) industrialisation. Subtitled "The Coming of the Machine as seen by contemporary observers", *Pandæmonium* is a collage of texts, any one of which demonstrates clear traces of the human "navigation" between faith, reason and the materials of the earth within recent history. Included in its pages, as a pertinent example here, might be a thoughtful little conceit from Samuel Butler's dystopian fantasy, *Erewhon* (1872), a novel inspired by a conjunction (like Ward's films, perhaps?) of the hot centres of European technological progress with an empty, antipodean hinterland: "In fact, wherever precision is required man flies to the machine at once...the machine is brisk and active, when the man is weary; it is clear-headed & collected, when the man is stupid and dull; it needs no slumber, when man must sleep or drop; ever at its post, ever ready for work, its alacrity never flags, its patience never gives in; its might is stronger than combined hundreds, and swifter than the flight of birds; it can burrow beneath the earth, and walk upon the largest rivers and sink not...Who shall say that man does see or hear? He is such a hive and swarm of parasites that it is doubtful whether his body is not more theirs than his, and whether he is anything but another kind of ant-heap after all. May not man himself become a sort of parasite upon the machines? An affectionate machine-tickling aphid?". Humphrey Jennings, *Pandæmonium 1660-1886: The Coming of the Machine as seen by contemporary observers*, edited by Mary-Lou Jennings and Charles Madge (London: André Deutsch, 1985): 328. Butler spent time in New Zealand in the late-1850s and early 1860s, and his novel, one of innumerable science fantasies published in the period, was subtitled "Over the Range", his two cultures from differing time zones being linked by a mountain crossing, rather than by a subterranean tunnel.

45 The script names him as the "Submarine Captain", but the words he is given are undiplomatic enough to suggest a symbolic, rather than a documentary, presence on the television screen.

46 The Cold War was still very centrally an issue when Ward planned and made his film in the mid-1980s, and the sea-monster queen-fish, which springs from Griffin's imagination, stands very obviously as harbinger and symptom of the ongoing 20th-century plague of nuclear proliferation, with its threat of both contamination and explosive devastation. However, the words of the "Submarine Captain" locate the theme into a very specific New Zealand context. It was the United States' presence in Vietnam which broadened

nuclear protest in New Zealand into a popular movement, one which, by the mid-1970s, had begun to question the country's involvement in the ANZUS defence alliance with Australia and the United States, an agreement which effectively guaranteed US military hegemony in the South Pacific. The focus of this protest centred on the visit of US naval vessels to New Zealand shores, and the fact that the US policy of "neither confirming nor denying" the presence of nuclear weaponry aboard such vessels merely served, in the eyes of New Zealanders, to illustrate the negligible significance that a small country appeared to have in the eyes of one of the major players, a feeling reinforced by similar patronising attitudes to New Zealand protests by two other nuclear powers, France and Great Britain: "that analogy was to do with New Zealand, which is a small place, isolated, trying to do something against a threat they see larger than themselves. Which in this case I saw as a nuclear thing." Ward, interview with Jimson. "If in doubt, keep it out!" ran a street slogan of the time. In 1984, the (then) left-of-centre Labour Party won election to government, with a nuclear-free programme as a central plank of its manifesto, and, within a year, the country's participation in ANZUS was effectively finished. New Zealand also provided a natural base for the Greenpeace movement in its moves to counter the insistent French nuclear testing in the Pacific, at Moruroa Atoll, and nothing could illustrate more clearly the contempt for national sovereignty by a big country towards a small one than the sinking of the movement's principal protest vessel, Rainbow Warrior, by French secret agents in Auckland Harbour in July 1985. "The script was actually written not very far from where the Rainbow Warrior was sunk, and at the same time". Ward, in "A Dialogue with Discrepancy": 10. By 1987, the government's anti-nuclear policy, including a total ban on visits by nuclear-powered or -armed vessels, had the support of more than 80% of the New Zealand population, and such support has remained consistent and persistent, the policy even being vigorously promulgated as an expanded nuclear-free Pacific by the leader of the right-wing National Party government in the 1990s. The Labour Prime Minister of the 1980s, David Lange, for whom the issue was very much part of a personal crusade, said at the time: "Our whole practical policy is a repudiation of nuclear deterrence". The comparative insignificance of New Zealand on the world map, both geographically and politically, meant perhaps that Lange could take a principled position unavailable to most other heads of state: "It's the will that matters. The answer to nuclear weapons lies in the reasons why governments put themselves in thrall to doctrines which essentially have it that nations can protect themselves by threatening to blow up the planet. It lies in knowing what breaks the spell that keeps governments from seeing that reliance on nuclear weapons is worse than foolish." See David Lange, *Nuclear Free: The New Zealand Way*

(Harmondsworth: Penguin Books, 1990): 8.

47 However, as the soundtrack of these images runs on, we hear mention of the pandemic of AIDS, and there is the hint of a broader sense of contemporary disaster. This slightly shotgun approach would seem to weaken the strength of the thematic argument, in that viral and other diseases prey on humankind much like the medieval plague, whereas nuclear contamination is indubitably the result of conscious human decision-making. One gets the sense that these moments had not been fully worked through by Ward. "But the nuclear thing was more important to me, certainly, than the Aids thing. And I also get very uneasy tying Aids in to the Black Death, anyway. I don't like doing it." Ward, in "A Dialogue with Discrepancy": 14.

48 The spire atop a cathedral was the highest man-made elevation in the medieval world, but "it served no practical architectural function – it was too narrow. Yet it symbolized a mix of pagan and Christian ideas – the aspirations of medieval belief, the use of church towers as military lookouts, and the setting up of spikes so that witches flying over would be impaled." Ward, in *The New Zealand Listener* 28 January 1989.

49 This is a sudden and brutal translation of the sceptical and commonsensical Searle to the mysteries of initiation, isolated between Heaven and Earth in the inverted position of purification, an image that belongs to primitive societies, just as it also refers to the twelfth card in the Tarot pack, and to both the practitioner, and process, of alchemy.

50 The wonderful commitment of Hamish McFarlane's performance here reaches its climax; absurdly, these scenes by the mountain lake were the first ones shot on location, and it was only McFarlane's second day in front of the cameras. The young actor carries the film, and it is to Ward's immense credit that he allows us so much time with the boy, establishing his simpleness, toughness, fierce will, terrors and, at this point in the film, intuitive grasp of what his own role has been in the unfolding of events, what it must now be, and the savage wisdom that lives in his innocence. It is a performance by a child actor that is remarkably without sentiment, against which the adults in the film seem, in comparison, quite childlike.

51 Quoted in Peter Hughes, "The Two Ages of the Navigator", *Cinema Papers* 72 (March 1989): 27.

52 In the essay, "The Day Panurge No Longer Makes People Laugh", in Milan Kundera, *Testaments Betrayed: An Essay in Nine Parts*,

translated by Linda Asher (London: HarperCollinsPublishers, 1996): 24.

[53] Phillip Adams, *The Weekend Australian* 11 June 1988.

[54] Jean Faydit de Terssac, "When Festival Juries Fail to Identify Genius", *Aspects de la France* 2 June 1988.

[55] Keith Connolly, *The Sydney Herald* 15 December 1988.

[56] Bill Collins, *The (Sydney) Daily Mirror* 8 December 1988.

[57] Nic., "The Navigator", *Variety* 11 May 1988.

[58] Sean French, "Antipodean time-travel", *The Observer* 21 August 1988: 37.

[59] Philip French, *The Observer* 29 May 1988: 39.

[60] Rob Lowing, *Sydney Sun Herald* 11 December 1988.

[61] Peter Crayford, "Epiphanies", *The Sydney Review* December 1988: 26-27.

[62] Derek Malcolm, "A World on Top", *The Guardian* 24 May 1988: 21.

[63] *Australian FilmNews* December 1988.

[64] Peter Mayer, "Meddling with the medieval", *Sunday Press* 18 December 1988.

[65] Michael Wilmington, "Firestorm and Dry Ice: The Cinema of Vincent Ward", *Film Comment* 29: 3 (May/June 1993): 51.

[66] Interview with Victor van Wetering, *Evening Post (Wellington)* 2 February 1989.

[67] Quoted in Hélène Cixous, *Three Steps on the Ladder of Writing*, translated by Sarah Cornell and Susan Sellers (New York: Columbia University Press, 1993): 107.

[68] Ibid: 107-108.

Credits

original title	The Navigator: A Mediaeval Odyssey
country of production	Australia/New Zealand
year of production	1988
length	87 minutes
gauge	35mm, colour and black-and-white
executive producer	Gary Hannam
producer	John Maynard
production company	Arenafilm / Film Investment Corporation of New Zealand
director	Vincent Ward
scriptwriter	Vincent Ward, Kely Lyons, Geoff Chapple
original idea	Vincent Ward
cinematographer	Geoffrey Simpson
composer	Davood A Tabrizi
editor	John Scott
art designer	Mike Becroft
production designer	Sally Campbell
costume designer	Glenys Jackson
main cast	Bruce Lyons (Connor), Chris Haywood (Arno), Hamish McFarlane (Griffin), Marshall Napier (Searle), Noel Appleby (Ulf), Paul Livingston (Martin), Sarah Peirse (Linnet), Mark Wheatley (Tog 1), Tony Herbert (Tog 2), Jessica Cardiff-Smith (Esme), Roy Wesney (Grandpa), Kathleen-Elizabeth Kelly (Grandma), Jay Saussey (Griffin's girlfriend), Charles Walker (Old Chrissie), Desmond Kelly (Smithy), Bill Le Marquand (Tom), Jay Lavea Laga'aia (Jay), Norman Fairley (Submarine Captain), Alister Babbage (Grigor).

Index